Streets of Highgate

© Camden History Society 2007

ISBN 978 0 904491 71 5

D1514078

Cover: Highgate High Street, looking towards
the Gatehouse (postcard c.1904). Left, The
Prince of Wales, then a beer retailer's; right,
the butcher's shop of Joseph Gurney Randall,
a successor to the Attkins family at No.82

Key

A The Gatehouse (p 7)
B The Dingle (p 63)
C Parkfield (p 68)
D St Michael's church (p 27)
E Hertford House (p 41)
F Lauderdale House (p 47)
G Holly Lodge (p 102)
H Traitor's Hill (p 106)
J Bromwich Walk (p 27)
K Kentish Town House (p 115)

Estates
1 Lord Southampton
2 Duke of St Albans
3 Earl of Mansfield

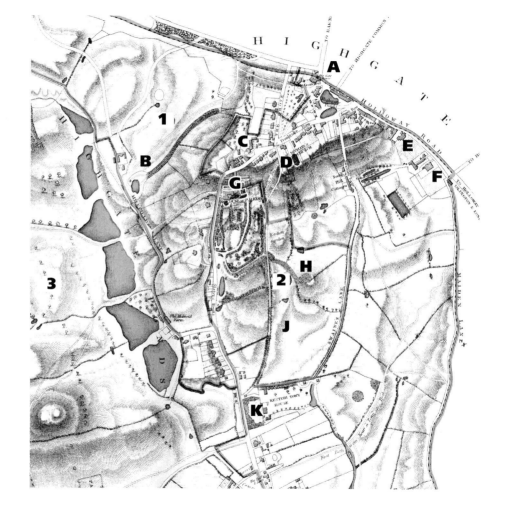

Detail of the Davies map, 1834:
the Highgate extremity of St Pancras parish

A survey of streets,
buildings & former residents
in a part of Camden

Streets of Highgate

Compiled by Camden History Society

Edited by Steven Denford and David A Hayes

Designed by Ivor Kamlish

General Editor of Camden History Society Publications F Peter Woodford

Diagram of the walks

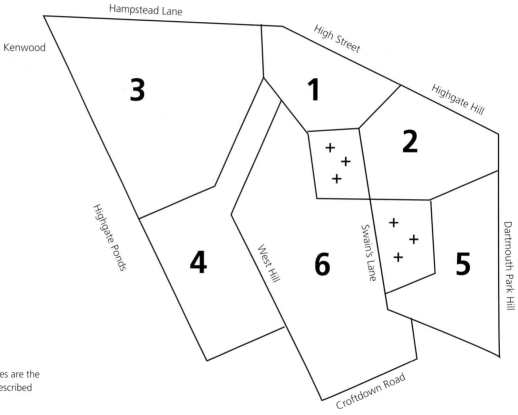

Hampstead Lane

High Street

Kenwood

Highgate Hill

3

1

2

Highgate Ponds

West Hill

Swain's Lane

Dartmouth Park Hill

4

6

5

Croftdown Road

Areas marked with a series of crosses are the
two parts of Highgate Cemetery, described
in a separate section (p 14)

Contents

List of illustrations and maps

Historical overview

Highgate proudly proclaims its location and purpose from the hilltop which commands an unrivalled prospect of the city lying at its foot. But this hill town was also a frontier town, and for many centuries a staging post of English history.

Although the name 'Highgate' came into general use in the 14th century, activity on the hilltop had begun soon after the Norman Conquest, when successive Bishops of London created a hunting park extending north from the site of the Gatehouse to a gate near the present Bald Faced Stag at East Finchley, and west to the Spaniards at Hampstead. Within the park, on what is now Highgate golf course, a residence was built at Lodge Hill, some traces of which still exist. Around the 'High Gate' itself, a few cottages would have marked the pioneer settlement. Most authorities agree that the gate gave the place its name, although some suggest it derives from the *gata* or road by the *haie* or hedge (of the Bishops' park).

The tensions following the Norman Conquest exposed the urgent need for improved communications between London and the rest of the country. In the 11th century, the main route to the North and Scotland seems to have been from Islington and Crouch End up Muswell Hill and onto Finchley Common. In winter and wet weather it was often impassable. So the Bishops 'upgraded' the access to their hunting park, using Maiden Lane (p 85), and forming a new road to the Gatehouse. Matthew Paris's best-known view of London in his itinerary from London to Rome of c.1250 suggests that it is based on the view from Highgate, which he would have passed en route from St Albans Abbey. At the gate into the Park, Bishop Richard de Newport was collecting tolls by 1318. The new road up Highgate Hill followed soon after, and the whole route through the park to Finchley was open by 1354, when a 'pavage' grant was authorised. Development was noticeable by 1381 and there may have been an element of planning. At the top of the hill, a hermit was established to maintain the road. This was the arrangement which was to last until 1535 when William Forte, the last hermit, was dispossessed.

The hamlet was now 'on the map'. The hermitage attracted pilgrim visitors, the hilltop was being cleared and modest houses began to define the High Street. Other visitors passed through the gate. King Richard II was led captive into London as the prisoner of Bolingbroke in 1399, and in 1461, during the Wars of the Roses, the Yorkist Thomas Thorpe, Baron of the Exchequer, was unlucky enough to be beheaded in Highgate by the rebellious Commons of Kent. Finchley Common and Highgate, on either side of the Park, now became military assembly points and staging posts for ceremonial entry into and exit from London. In 1483, the 12-year-old Edward V was welcomed here by the Lord Mayor of London and escorted to the Tower, not as was proclaimed to his coronation, but to his death later the same year, possibly on the orders of Richard III. After Richard's death at Bosworth Field, Henry VII received a similar welcome at Highgate at the start of his longer and more distinguished reign.

Perhaps the most exciting century at Highgate was about to begin. By 1500, available records indicate the progress that had been made in the development of the settlement. In 1530, Cantelowes Manor, in which part of Highgate village lay, found it necessary to appoint a separate Constable for Highgate. By 1552 five taverns were recorded, including the predecessor of the Angel or Salutation, the Gatehouse and the Swan, and as well as the houses lining the High Street more ambitious houses were being built away from the road. Sir Roger Cholmeley's house of 1530 was home to the first eminent resident and the highest taxpayer in St Pancras parish; he was founder and benefactor of the school that was to perpetuate his name. Upon the school's establishment in 1565, the chapel

1 Highgate Old Chapel, by H A Gillman (Wallis Bequest)

of the hermit was rebuilt [1] for use by the growing hamlet, which adopted it as an unofficial chapel-of-ease.

Elizabeth Tudor's first recorded visit was an occasion for prayer rather than cheers. The Princess Elizabeth had been ordered to London by Queen Mary, her half-sister, after the failure of Sir Thomas Wyatt's revolt. Elizabeth had been living at Ashridge and was ill enough to be carried in a litter. Her journey took eleven days, Elizabeth 'lingering' in the village en route. Four uneasy years later she returned to London in triumph in a mounted victory parade of 1000 nobles. She visited Highgate several times in her long reign, staying at Sir William Cornwallis' magnificent Arundel House, completed in Armada year 1588. Such royal patronage encouraged other visitors and residents. Norden, writing in 1593, commended it as "a most pleasant dwelling, yet not so pleasant as healthful. Many people who come here sick were cured by the sweet salutarie air". James I stayed at Arundel House in 1603 on his way from Scotland to his coronation.

The next 100 years were to see the building of some of Highgate's finest houses as well as creating the line of the High Street as it is today. In the English Civil War (1642-49) the village was spared actual conflict, but it experienced the religious and social polarisation that accompanied the rise of Puritanism and nonconformity. Some Roman Catholics remained as 'refugees' until 1651, when, after Lord Arundel made a public profession of Protestantism, they moved elsewhere. The Puritan City of London ensured that Highgate, a strategic outpost on the Great North Road, was secured for the Parliament, and this interest was reinforced during the Civil War and the years of the Commonwealth. The Protectorate ended in 1660 when General Monck's Scottish army, 5,800 strong, marched through the village to London. Charles II regained his throne and the Duke of Lauderdale his house. Very strong tradition connects the 'Merry Monarch' and his mistress Nell Gwynne with the house. The Duke left by 1679, leading a gradual retreat of the nobility from the hilltop.

In spite of the severity of the Restoration settlement for Nonconformists, it was, for Highgate, a shot in the arm. The village lay outside the five-mile limit within which only Church of England worship was allowed, and thus attracted Dissenters who took full advantage of their new home. Many were City merchants, including Sir William Ashurst and the Protestant fundamentalist William Blake, whose generous but ill-supported 'Ladies Hospital' so tragically failed. Their main legacy is the number of handsome, solid houses which still stand in the village, and give it the appearance of a small town.

The southern slopes of the hill were still open fields. Arable cultivation gave way to grass for hay and pasture after 1600, which may have limited the population growth. One activity that did increase with the general growth of London was droving. From the 14th century onwards, Highgate saw the regular passage of sheep and cattle from Wales and the North, on the hoof, to the London markets. They came through the gate in their thousands, to water at the pubs and the ponds. Drovers who wished to avoid the toll took advantage of the track that led across fields below Cane Wood or Kenwood and which was to become present-day Millfield Lane in its lower reaches.

If the 17th century had witnessed the flow and ebb of aristocratic residence, the 18th was the age of the merchants and the high point of Highgate's history to date. Although the guards marched north to deal with Bonnie Prince Charlie in 1745, and the Cambridge Militia was stationed here in the aftermath of the Gordon Riots, the country as a whole was more settled. The town attracted rich residents, as advertisements for property confirm, and with the establishment of the turnpike in 1717, the roads were improved for City workers and summer visitors. Although many long-distance coaches passed through, they seem to have been little used by local travellers, but highway robbery, a sure measure of increased traffic and wealth, became a serious problem at the foot of the hill. Evening patrols were introduced and an anti-robbery fund started. The road up the hill was widened in 1767, trees were felled and pavements levelled. Finally, in 1774, Highgate obtained its badge of status, its own Lighting and Watching Act. It was now a real town with assemblies, a theatre and a flourishing social life, quite independent of the two parishes whose jurisdiction it shared. Prominent local landowners included the Earls of Mansfield and the Fitzroys (Barons Southampton) who owned large estates on the western fringes of the town.

The first years of the 19th century in Highgate were dominated by the planned construction of the Archway Road. The first scheme collapsed, with its tunnel, in 1812, to the delight of High Street traders and publicans who rightly surmised it would take away, or at least diminish their livelihood. The second attempt, by Thomas Telford, was successful and the toll road was opened in 1813. At this time Highgate had 19 licensed taverns, and they were the first to feel the draught once coach traffic eventually moved to the easier route (the new road proved unpopular for some time).

In 1809, the 21-acre Coutts estate began its distinguished and benevolent career, and to the west, villas were appearing on the fields owned by the Fitzroys, sporadically at first but more consistently after 1840 when their Highgate lands were divided up and sold at auction on a single day. The year before, the grounds of Ashurst House had become Highgate Cemetery, which acquired an eastward extension in 1854. Together with the grounds of St Pancras Infirmary on Dartmouth Park Hill these properties provided a 'cordon sanitaire' against the relentless northward march of bricks and mortar which would culminate in the presumption of 'Highgate New Town'.

Up in the town itself, a legal challenge to the governors of the free school had important repercussions. The Eldon judgement concluded that the school's long-time support of the unofficial chapel-of-ease had become prejudicial to the educational objectives of the school, which was in a poor way. The chapel was closed and replaced by a proper parish church whose spire was to give the hilltop new distinction, and also marked the final severing of the old ecclesiastical link with the parish of St Pancras. A few years later, the school appointed a new headmaster, John Bradley Dyne, who lifted it out of the doldrums and expanded it greatly.

Other links with St Pancras suffered at this time. In the early years of the St Pancras Vestry, the well-to-do residents had been nobility and were treated with respect. Vestry meetings were frequently held in the Flask. But when in 1819 democracy in St Pancras was hijacked by the formation of a self-perpetuating 'closed' Vestry, Highgate no longer wanted, or was not invited, to be part of the stormy happenings far off in Camden Town. Moreover, with the closure of the White Lion and its theatre the place became less lively for visitors, even more so when both church and chapel mounted an attack on Sunday trading. The situation was partly redeemed by the emergence in 1839 of the Highgate Literary and Scientific Institution, whose lectures and lending library continue to be much appreciated.

Piped water arrived in 1850 and the last pond was filled in 1864. Pond Square became an official open space in 1885. With the abolition of the turnpikes, the payment of the Bishop's Toll at the 'High Gate' ceased in 1876. Highgate, as we have seen, had often been a retreat for refugees, religious and political. In 1816 it became the final home of the poet Coleridge, and for 18 years a centre for literary pilgrims. Their favourite leafy walks revealed the 'retreat potential' of the Hampstead Heath boundary, where luxury homes, suitably camouflaged, superseded farms and cottages later in the century.

Although there had been an hourly local coach service to the City for some years, the opening of the Archway bypass did little to help local travellers. The railway, too, was late. Not until 1867 did the Edgware, Highgate and London railway reach its station at the bottom of Southwood Lane. Once again, severe gradients, a poor service and a 100-ft climb were to deter an excess of newcomers. Perhaps the mediocre trains created enthusiasm for the unique cable tramway which traversed Highgate Hill from the Archway Tavern from 1884 to 1909.

Because of its healthy reputation, many schools were attracted to the town, where the spacious merchants' houses offered suitable accommodation. Two developments of the 1880s provided welcome additional houses for the middle classes when Winchester Hall and Bisham House were demolished, and Highgate's green space was increased in 1889 when Sir Sydney Waterlow presented his 29-acre estate to the new London County Council as a "garden for the gardenless".

1900 was notable for the building of two small blocks of mansion flats in Pond Square, a portent for the future. In the previous year, the St Pancras side of Highgate became an integral part of the new Metropolitan Borough which in 1906 was to build its first public library in Highgate New Town. With its 'green belt' intact, the village, with its highly structured society and sporting, horticultural and intellectual organisations, set about enjoying the remaining years of peace. The cable tramway was taken over by the LCC and reopened in 1910 with a direct service to Moorgate. Three years previously the Hampstead Tube had reached the Archway Tavern, offering easy access to the West End, and by 1914 some regular omnibus services had been extended to the village.

WWI took a grievous toll of young men from the close-knit community, as can be seen from the various memorials. At home, the residents of Fairseat were persuaded by the Government to vacate the house for the duration in favour of aristocratic refugees, and the peace of Holly Village was disturbed by a small bomb from a German Gotha. Allotments were provided in Waterlow Park for growing food.

In 1922 and 1923 the Coutts estate was sold off and subsequently filled with mock-Tudor houses and flats, although some of the original planting was retained. Farther down the hill, St Pancras Council constructed the architecturally superior Brookfield Estate. In 1934, the battle lines were drawn again with the demolition of historic South Grove House in favour of 50 rather unsympathetic flats. Protests were met with bland assurances that residents would "respect the neighbours", which at that time could not be enforced. Not far away, on Highgate Hill, Cholmeley Lodge was similarly replaced by a large block of flats by the same architect which, deplored at the time, has proved far more successful. Highgate acquired in the 1930s several other high-profile modern movement icons such as Highpoint 1 and 2 (along North Road in Haringey and therefore outside the scope of this book). It has remained a popular home for architects, whose more modest houses, often built on backland sites, display design standards of a very high order.

As the decade progressed, trams were supplanted by trolley buses, and the Underground was extended through Highgate to Mill Hill and Barnet. In 1939 the BBC built a telecommunications mast to relay signals for its new wonder invention, TV, at the top of Swain's Lane. Television was extinguished during the war years, and the mast was used to broadcast the Home Service and Light Programme radio networks. It played another important part in the war effort, by picking up the frequency used by German aeroplanes and jamming their system, thereby thwarting many of their raids. Highgate School was evacuated to Westward Ho! and Channing School to Ross-on-Wye, their premises being taken over by the military. War damage in the village was slight and mostly resulted from a flying bomb which fell in Waterlow Park in 1944 close to the underground shelters. Further south, damage and casualties had come to Highgate Road and Highgate New Town in 1941.

Evacuees and grateful survivors returned in 1945, but lingering post-war shortages restricted repairs and redevelopment in the village. This was fortunate, given the lack of planning protection then in place. But with the introduction of Listing Controls in 1962 a long schedule of buildings in Highgate received statutory protection for the first time. In the very same year the first major blow was struck by the Conservative Minister of Transport, Ernest Marples. He sought to solve the bottleneck that the Archway Road had become by making the historic route up the hill to North Road a designated 'Lorry Route'. In spite of vehement protests, this policy remained in place for a further 13 years. The most significant reaction was the formation of the Highgate Society, and the designation of the village by both Camden and Haringey as a 'Conservation Area' under the Civic Amenities Act 1967. Protests were kept up, and in 1974, 300 local residents halted all traffic in the High Street for an hour. A ban on heavy lorries came into force the next year.

While public opinion was occupied in protecting the High Street, development of a very different order was proceeding in Highgate New Town. Much of the housing was in need of extensive restoration, and under the financial guidelines then in force, it was cheaper to rebuild than to repair. So, between 1972 and 1981, Camden rebuilt a large part of the area. In line with changing fashions, the early bold concrete terraces gave way in later stages to more homely brickwork and the rehabilitation of the remaining original terraces, all carried out with care and flair.

Yet another key site at this time was Highgate Cemetery. It had been in decline since 1920. The private company owners had sold off every asset possible when, at Easter 1975, they suddenly closed it down. Within a few months the 'Friends of Highgate Cemetery' had been formed to draw up plans for its conservation. Little

by little this extraordinary place of rest is regaining its dignity as a result of most dedicated effort, much of it voluntary.

What of the future? One subject has concerned the village for many years: the well-being of the High Street and its traders. Highgate has a very long tradition of local traders whose families have served the place well, in some cases for over a century. The first, and so far only, chain store arrived but recently. Times change, and it is probably true that it is no longer possible to buy everything desired by today's voracious consumers in the High Street...but does that matter? Also, thirteen estate agents in such a small area does seem a trifle excessive. In the past, Highgate may have had a tendency to resist 'changing with the times', but who can blame it when, thanks to its own efforts, there is still so much of historical interest and grace to see and experience?

So, as we explore this very individual and independent corner of Camden, we should be grateful to all those who have been and still are inspired to care so diligently for their local environment. To paraphrase John Philpot Curran in 1790, "the condition of environmental conservation, like that of Liberty, is eternal vigilance".

Boundaries

Highgate developed on both sides of a boundary formed by the High Street and a line running west from the Gatehouse a few yards south of Hampstead Lane (whose present route was formed in the 1790s). To the north and east of the High Street lay the old parish of St Mary, Hornsey and the Bishop of London's Manor; to the south and west, the parish of St Pancras. The south-western area is the subject of this book.

This side of Highgate was included in the County of London from 1889, becoming part of St Pancras Metropolitan Borough in 1900 and of the London Borough of Camden in 1965. The north-eastern half remained in Middlesex, administered by the Hornsey Local Board from 1867 to 1903 and thereafter by Hornsey Borough Council until 1965, when it became part of the London Borough of Haringey. The Haringey side of the High Street and Highgate Hill, as well as the Camden side, are described in Routes 1 & 2, otherwise the picture of this historic thoroughfare would be incomplete. The slopes south of Hornsey Lane, to the east of Dartmouth Park Hill, which are sometimes described as

'Highgate', are in the Borough of Islington, and are not included here, although we do chart the history of St Joseph's church and the Whittington Hospital.

The part of Highgate that was historically within St Pancras parish was split between the northernmost parts of two manors, Tottenhall and Cantelowes, as shown on the diagram. Both manors were 'prebendal', endowing Canons of St Paul's, absentee landlords who leased land to others under a system known as 'copyhold'. A copyhold lease was one given by the lord of the manor (in this case the prebendary) during the lives of three named persons. Two copies were usually made, one for the lord and one for the tenant, who, provided he paid his rents and fines, and met other obligations, enjoyed what amounted to hereditary tenure. The prebendal stalls in St Paul's Cathedral remain to this day to remind us of the existence of these manors. Most of Highgate village itself lay within Cantelowes manor. By the 19th century, its manorial lands south of the village had passed into the hands of several landowners, including the Coutts family, the Earls of Dartmouth and Harry Chester. We meet these estates in our explorations in Routes 5 & 6. All these lands were gradually converted into freeholds by the process of buying out the copyhold interest, a form of tenure only finally abolished in 1922.

Tottenhall manor lands, which stretched south to Tottenham Court, lay west of West Hill. The manor had been acquired by the Fitzroy family when Henry Fitzroy, an illegitimate son of Charles II, married Isabella, Countess of Arlington.

Henry's grandson, the soldier Charles Fitzroy, was able, in 1768, to convert his leaseholds into freeholds by special Act of Parliament, aided by his elder brother, the Duke of Grafton, then effectively prime minister. Charles became Baron

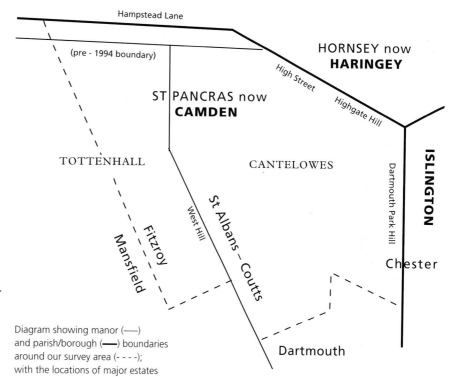

Diagram showing manor (——) and parish/borough (——) boundaries around our survey area (- - - -); with the locations of major estates

Southampton in 1780, and the Fitzroys' property was subsequently known as the Southampton estate. The Fitzroy family lived for some decades in a large villa on the former demesne lands of the manor, in a part of Highgate now known as Fitzroy Park. To the west their grounds abutted Kenwood, owned from the mid-18th century by the Murray family, later Earls of Mansfield, along with woods and farmland to the south as far as Parliament Hill Fields. When the Southampton estate was auctioned off for building in 1840, the Earl of Mansfield secured a large portion of the land to ensure there was no development on his estate. When his successor in the early 20th century decided it was time to build over the estate, prominent inhabitants of what had been the Fitzroys' lands managed to thwart his plans so that the western edge of Highgate still maintains its verdant outlook. This area is dealt with in Routes 3 and 4.

A diagram of the six routes is on p 4.

Highgate Cemetery

By the early 19th century, inner-city churchyards (mostly the graveyards around churches) were unable to cope with the number of burials and were seen as a hazard to health and an undignified way to treat the dead. This provided an incentive to provide large, private cemeteries in a ring round the outside of London. The entrepreneurs of the funeral business (joint stock companies) prospered until challenged later in the century by the emergence of municipal cemeteries and the legalisation of cremation.

Highgate was the third of the three cemeteries the London Cemetery Company was authorised to build by a Parliamentary Act of 1836, the other two being Kensal Green and Norwood. Of the three, Highgate has the best, or at least the most romantic, buildings. The original ones are by Stephen Geary, architect and founder of the company; the later ones are by J B Bunning, the surveyor who was appointed in 1839. Landscape design was the work of David Ramsay; his layout not only had to solve the problems of a steeply sloping site but also take account of the existing trees in what had been the fields and orchard of

Ashurst House. For £3,500, the Company obtained a 17-acre site. Today that site, the **West Ground**, contains 51,000 burial plots and is the last resting place of 166,800 souls.

The cemetery was consecrated by the Bishop of London on 20 May 1839. Two acres in the north-east corner were left unconsecrated (for Dissenters and others), being tactfully hidden by a row of chestnut trees. Highgate was soon seen as London's equivalent to Père Lachaise in Paris. Like the other new cemeteries, it quickly became a fashionable place for burials and was much admired and visited. At first, visitors came to enjoy the magnificent views over London [2] as much as the artistry of the memorials. "In such a place the aspect of death is softened" wrote *The Lady* in 1850. Local residents had initially disapproved of the cemetery, but once tickets were issued to walk in the grounds they came to regard it as a local amenity.

Stephen Geary died in 1854, and in 1865 so did the secretary of the company, who was found to have embezzled funds on a large scale. But the cemetery was thriving, its reputation visibly enhanced by the principal attendant of the West Ground in his dark green knee-length gold-braided jacket and top hat.

By 1920 the cemetery was a declining asset. After WWII its nurseries were sold, and properties along Swain's Lane were abandoned. In 1960, the London

Cemetery Company became part of United Cemeteries and the main administration was transferred to Nunhead Cemetery. At Easter 1975, United Cemeteries declared the West Ground closed and locked the gates. There was an immediate protest, and in October the Friends of Highgate Cemetery (FOHC) was formed. The GLC General Powers Act 1976 provided for the acquisition of the whole cemetery by the London Borough of Camden, who provided grants to the owners for a number of years. FOHC obtained leave to undertake limited clearance of undergrowth, voluntarily. But Camden eventually declined to purchase. In 1981 the owners decided to sell for £50 to Pinemarsh Ltd, a company formed by two members of the FOHC, a solicitor and an accountant, to safeguard the future of the cemetery. The ownership was later transferred to the Highgate Cemetery Charity (HCC). The policy of the Friends who manage the cemetery was, and is, to preserve the character of the grounds by maintaining the buildings, monuments and vegetation in a state of 'managed neglect'. A landscape plan was drawn up by Jenny Cox, assisted by architects Caröe & Martin. "Our aim", it declares, "must be that the nineteenth century celebration of death should become a twentieth (and twenty-first) century celebration of Life", a justification perhaps for our including these streets of the dead in this book.

2 View of London from a newly opened Highgate Cemetery, showing the Circle of Lebanon (Heal Collection)

For the visitor, the main highlights of the West Ground include the Grade-I-Listed Egyptian Avenue with its monumental archway flanked by obelisks and bulbous columns leading past tombs with massive iron doors to the Circle of Lebanon with its tapering doorways and heavy classical pediments. To the north, and above, towers the finely crafted monument to Julius Beer, proprietor of *The Observer*, designed by J Oldrid Scott in 1876. Just behind are the Catacombs, tomb

cloisters inserted below the terrace which survives from Ashurst House, and which, before the vegetation took over, provided a convincing link between the parishioners of St Michael's and their departed.

Entrance to the West Ground is by guided tour only but in this way one can

help the FOHC in its herculean task.
One is led along the winding main paths
flanked by the brick-lined tombs of the
rich of Victorian England and up to the
architectural highlights of the cemetery.
The tour takes in some of the amazing
variety of styles of grave, nearly fifty of
which are Listed. John Betjeman dubbed
the cemetery a "Victorian Valhalla" and
it is easy to see why. Unusual monuments
include the sleeping lion on the tomb of
the menagerist George Wombwell; the bull
mastiff guarding his master, the pugilist
Tom Sayers; the furniture-making Maple
family grave resembling a six-poster bed;
the elegant Grecian day-bed for novelist
Mrs Henry Wood; and the Art-Deco
Hartley monument, topped with a huge
urn and bearing hieroglyphics. A stumped
cricket wicket adorns the gravestone of the
sports goods manufacturer Alfred Prosser.

The list of notable people in the West
Ground is long, and space dictates that we
can mention only a few. Among writers are
Radclyffe Hall and Christina Rossetti; there
are numerous architects such as Edward
Blore, J B Bunning, Stephen Geary, E
B Lamb, and S S Teulon; the locksmith
Charles Chubb; Charles Cruft, founder
of the eponymous dog show; the scientist
Michael Faraday; the opera impresario
Carl Rosa; the 'Brothers Dalziel', prolific
wood engravers; and the actor Patrick
Wymark. But many paupers were also
buried here, including young children from
the Foundling Hospital, probably because
Bunning was on its Board.

In 1862 Dante Gabriel Rossetti buried
his young wife Lizzie Siddal, the Pre-
Raphaelites' model, in the Rossetti family's
plot. He placed a collection of manuscript
poems in her hair, an action he thought
better of seven years later when he had the
grave re-opened so he could publish them.
Stories associated with the cemetery are
many. For example, there is "the man who
never was". Thomas Druce was buried
here in 1864 but his family subsequently
claimed he had never existed, being an
alter ego of the ultra-reclusive 5th Duke of
Portland. Their claim to the latter's estate
was eventually disproved by an exhumation
in 1907. Then there is the more recent
story of a vampire that gained ground after
a group of young occultists began roaming
around the dilapidated cemetery in the late
1960s. A mass vampire hunt took place
on Friday 13 March 1970 amidst much
press and TV publicity. Shortly before
this, scenes in Hammer's *Taste the Blood of
Dracula* were filmed here.

The work of the FOHC in recent years
has helped to counteract uncontrolled
growth in the West Ground. The cemetery
is now a natural, woodland park, with
a special beauty and charm, full of old-
growth trees, shrubbery and wildflowers
that are a haven for birds and small animals
like foxes. Highgate Cemetery has to be
experienced and felt at first hand ... and
there are still limited opportunities for
new interments. One recent interment
in the West Ground was of the ex-KGB
officer Alexander Litvinenko, mysteriously
poisoned in 2006.

So successful was the original cemetery
that an extension was soon necessary. A
further 20-acre site was acquired on the
opposite side of Swain's Lane, comprising
the western part of the former Abbot's
Barn Field on the Chester estate and,
bordering the road, a narrow sloping field
called The Slip. After the opening of the
East Ground in 1855, the existing chapels
flanking the West Ground gatehouse served
the new cemetery too. A hydraulic bier lift
was installed in the left-hand (Anglican)
chapel to lower coffins into a tunnel
leading under Swain's Lane.

After the West Ground closed in 1975,
the East Ground was kept going for some
years by Camden Council before passing
ownership to Pinemarsh, and later the
HCC. Though similarly sylvan and often
overgrown, it is still a working cemetery,
and is sometimes temporarily closed during
funerals. Otherwise, it is open daily and,
on payment of a modest entry fee, you may
wander at will.

Just inside the gate, three classical
mausoleums in red granite house the
remains of three wealthy gentlemen:
Donald Smith, later Lord Strathcona
& Mount Royal (d.1914), the Scottish-
Canadian fur trapper turned financier and

politician who promoted the completion of the Canadian Pacific Railway; Thomas Pocklington (d.1935), the generous benefactor of services to the blind; and Lord Dalziel (d.1928), who introduced the motor-cab to London.

The mausoleums form the only architecture of note in the East Ground, but there are numerous interesting graves. Invest further in a leaflet showing the locations of the most noteworthy. Of the 850 Highgate grave occupants said to be 'notable', over 350 feature in the *Dictionary of National Biography*. Sir Leslie Stephen (d.1904), co-editor of the dictionary's first 26 volumes, and the father of Virginia Woolf, lies buried up a minor path to the left, just beyond the mausoleums.

Beside the main path on the right is the grave of William Foyle (d.1963), the founder of the famous bookshop. Ahead, the left-hand fork leads towards the cemetery's much visited north-east corner. Notice en route, and set back on the right, the aptly unworked headstone of Richard ('Stoney') Smith (d.1900), the miller from Stone in Staffordshire whose patented way of treating wheatgerm was central to the production of Hovis bread.

Tucked away up a nearby side path is the grave of the novelist George Eliot, buried here in 1880 under her eventual married name, Mary Ann Cross. Beside her lies her long-time lover and cohabitee,

the writer George Henry Lewes (d.1878). Alongside him lies George Holyoake (d.1906), the Chartist, co-operator and pioneer secularist.

Unmissable nearby is the cemetery's most visited spot, the very conspicuous monument to Karl Marx. At his funeral in 1883, at which Engels spoke, only twenty people were present, and the grave was modest, as Marx had wished. Lenin came to visit it on several of his trips to London. Relocated to a more prominent spot, and surmounted by Laurence Bradshaw's iconic bronze portrait head of 1956, commissioned by the Communist Party of Great Britain, the grave became a place of pilgrimage for numerous Communist delegations. Pilgrims included the Russian leaders Kruschev and Bulganin in 1956, the cosmonaut Valeri Bykovsky in 1967 and the gymnast Olga Korbut seven years later. Not all visitors have been admirers. In the early hours of Sunday 18 January 1970 an extremist group attempted to blow up the monument with explosives; they daubed swastikas and tried to hack off Marx's nose. In July 1974 further extremists succeeded in toppling his head from its plinth.

Opposite the Marx monument is the tomb of the philosopher Herbert Spencer (d.1903), the pioneer of evolutionary theory who was the first to use the term "survival of the fittest". Beside Marx lies Claudia Jones (d.1964), the communist

black freedom campaigner who founded the Notting Hill Carnival.

To the north is an area occupied mostly by relatively recent graves, including those of the comedian Max Wall (d.1990) and of the controversial artist Feliks Topolski (d.1986), one of the many Poles buried in this corner of the East Ground.

Although most of the notable graves are here at the northern end, there are others in the lower reaches that are well worth a visit. There, not far from the now disused Chester Road gate, William Henry Betty, the once famous child actor (d.1874) lies in a tomb of his own design. You may like to seek out the elusive grave, in the cemetery's south-west extremity, of William Henry Monk (d.1889), choirmaster, organist, and composer of the hymn tune *Eventide*, better known as *Abide with Me*.

As you follow the central pathway back up to the main entrance, don't miss on the right a stone grand piano marking the grave of Harry Thornton (d.1918), a pianist, singer and imitator said to have entertained the troops during WWI. Farther up, on the same right-hand side of the path, is the grave of the actor Sir Ralph Richardson (d.1983), while a left turn at the top leads past that of theatre architect Frank Matcham (d.1920). Bear further left to end your visit, perhaps, at Edwin Lutyens' Gothic monument to the pioneer cinematographer William Friese-Greene (d.1921).

Present street names and their origins

? = speculative or doubtful
† = no known specific local connection

Highgate is no local cemetery: its grave occupants have come from far and wide. After his death in 2001, the ashes of Douglas Adams, author of *The Hitchhiker's Guide to the Galaxy*, were brought from California for interment here. *Local* residents whom we encounter in the course of our walks who were eventually laid to rest in Highgate Cemetery include Sir William Henry Bodkin, Jacob Bronowski, James and Herbert Cutbush, Dame Frances Gardner, Sir John Glover, Oscar Lewis, John Lloyd, Walter Neurath, Jonathan Payne, Sir James Pennethorne, Sir Henry Purey-Cust, John Rock, and James Yates; and the sometime owner of neighbouring Holly Lodge, the 9th Duke of St Albans.

Angel
Eponymous tavern adjoins

Bacon's
Francis, lawyer, politician & philosopher, died at Arundel House, 1626

Balmore
Name of several Scottish villages †

Bank
Raised roadway

Bisham
Bisham House stood on site

Bertram
Origin unknown

Broadbent
Thomas, local C19 builder

Bromwich
Thomas, C18 paper merchant & landowner

Brookfield
Meadow traversed by River Fleet

Chester
Harry, C19 civil servant, HLSI president & local landowner

Colva
Colfa, a Radnorshire village? (see p 94)

Croftdown
Croft Lodge, at road's west end

Dartmouth Park
C19 development on the Earl of Dartmouth's estate

Doynton
Gloucestershire village? (see p 92)

Fitzroy
Family name of the Lords Southampton, C18/C19 landowners

Grove
A plantation or avenue of trees

Hampstead
Leading to the neighbouring village

Haversham
Buckinghamshire village?

Hexagon
Comprises 6 houses, though rectangularly arranged

Highfields
Self-explanatory

Highgate
Probably, the medieval tollgate
erected by Bishop of London

Hillway
Self-explanatory

Holly
A plant which thrives locally

Holly Lodge
C19 house & grounds

Kingswear
Devonshire village opposite
Dartmouth (cf. Dartmouth Park)

Langbourne
City of London ward, location of
Coutts' bank's first branch?

Lulot
Blended forenames of Carter family
members? (see Retcar & p 89)

Makepeace
Origin unknown

Merton
Oxford college attended
by 2nd son of Meaburn Tatham,
the builder of Merton Lodge

Millfield
Meadow adjoining a medieval mill

Oakeshott
John, C19 doctor and HLSI member

Pond
Village ponds, long drained & filled in

Raydon
Suffolk village near Ipswich,
Harry Chester's birthplace

Retcar
Anagram of Carter,
surname of C19 landowners

Robin
The red-breasted bird,
evoking a rural past

St Anne's
Mother of the Virgin,
dedicatee of neighbouring church

St Albans
9th Duke of,
early owner of Holly Lodge

Sandstone
Sand-coloured concrete,
a feature of the Whittington Estate

Stoneleigh
Village in Warwickshire? †

Swain's
Swineherd's

Townsend
James Townshend [sic],
local C19 builder

West Hill
The more westerly of two ascents

Winscombe
Somerset village? †

Witanhurst
Mansion of Sir Arthur Crosfield, MP;
from Anglo-Saxon for
'parliament' and 'wooded hill'

Route 1
Highgate Village
Circular walk from The Gatehouse
For modern map see back cover

Our route begins and ends at the historic crossroads and tollgate that gave the village its purpose and probably its name.

From one of the several bus stops – in Pond Square, at the 'South Grove' stop in Highgate High Street or in Highgate West Hill – walk towards the Gatehouse tavern and stand on the corner by the flower stall facing the inn.

The Gatehouse is on the site of the oldest recorded structure in the village. At the beginning of the 14th century, a new route from London to the North was created when a toll road (now North Road/North Hill in Haringey) was made through the Bishop of London's Hornsey Park. Tolls were being levied here in 1318, and an archway was subsequently built over the roadway through which all south- or northbound vehicles had to pass and pay a toll. Southwood Lane, leading north-eastwards to Muswell Hill is recorded in 1601. Hampstead Lane (p 52), on the other hand, ran westward to Hampstead village, and is part of an earlier route through the Bishop's park. The road running south-westwards downhill, an extension of Highgate West Hill, was the medieval route

from Kentish Town, here following the western boundary of Cantelowes Manor. Its eastern boundary is formed by the road that became Highgate Hill and High Street – the dividing line between the parishes of St Pancras and St Mary Hornsey, and now between the London Boroughs of Camden and of Haringey. As befits a hilltop settlement, the crossroads are at the highest point (427 ft, 130m).

The name 'Highgate' first appears in 1354, in connection with the road to the gateway and the hermits who lived nearby and repaired the road. A decade later, William Phelippe is recorded as a Hermit in Royal Grant for collecting tolls. With the increase in traffic, a hamlet rapidly grew up here, possibly planned. The reputation of the hermits also grew. Their task of repairing the roads must have been unending. 'Miracles' were reported in 1464, and papal indulgences were issued in support of the chapel built nearby. The hermit, John Cledro at this time, was responsible for celebrating mass, repairing the roads and burying those murdered by robbers. The parish churches of Hornsey and St Pancras were a long walk in either direction, and the hermits' chapel soon became a place of pilgrimage and an unofficial 'chapel-of-ease'.

This was most irregular, and on 28 May 1503 an incident occurred that was to be repeated in one form or another many times during the next three centuries.

The vicar of St Pancras and parishioners were beating the bounds of their parish, and came into conflict with Thomas Walterkyne, hermit of St Michael beside Highgate. A brawl ensued, and the matter was referred to the Court of Star Chamber, but its verdict has not survived. By 1565, the chapel was a ruin, and the hermits a memory. The chapel was rebuilt in 1571 and 1578 and enlarged in 1616, 1628 and 1719, being finally superseded by the new church of St Michael in South Grove in 1832. Illustrations show the old chapel to have been a curious structure, with a small tower and spire ([1], p 8). The present building, which has stood on its site since 1867, is the chapel of **Highgate School**.

The school was founded by Sir Roger Cholmeley in 1565. Highgate School, today, lies almost entirely within Haringey, and we shall not be exploring its many buildings, but its influence on the development of the village cannot be overlooked. Sir Roger Cholmeley was appointed Chief Justice of the King's Bench in 1552, but was committed to the Tower in the following year by Catholic Queen Mary for having witnessed the will of her Protestant half-brother Edward VI. On his release, he settled in Highgate, living in a house on the site of the later Fairseat (p 41). He applied to found a school in 1562, and letters patent were issued in 1565, two months before he died. The Bishop of London had granted him the Chapel Field on which stood the ruins of the hermits' chapel, and also a windmill. His work was continued by the six governors whom he had appointed. These had to be residents of Highgate, and in practice were prominent citizens of the City of London. The school was to be a free school for 40 scholars from Highgate, Holloway, Hornsey, Finchley and Kentish Town.

After the rebuilding of the chapel, the school governors laid down rules, followed for the next two centuries, which stipulated that the chapel was intended for local residents as well as scholars; the schoolmaster was also the Reader of the Chapel. Increasingly, the school funds were used by the governors to maintain the chapel and for poor relief. The chapel was licensed for marriages in 1616, and in its role as chapel-of-ease was regularly enlarged to cater for the increasing population. Meanwhile, the education of the 40 scholars suffered. In 1819 it was found that they were being taught by the sexton, while the inhabitants were clamouring for further improvements to the chapel. The powers of the governors were challenged, and in 1827 Lord Chancellor Eldon delivered a judgement which reversed their priorities: the governors were not bound to enlarge the chapel, its use as a chapel-of-ease was unlawful, and a new chapel for Highgate would have to be built elsewhere. The special Highgate Act of 1830 for the construction of St

Michael's church ended the traditional responsibilities and privileges of the vicar and church trustees of St Pancras, despite their vociferous protests. The school was to be re-established as a grammar school under new statutes: 40 free places were to be retained, but the Master could take as many fee-paying students as he liked. This may have saved the school, which by 1838 had only 18 pupils, though it excluded local boys who did not possess the academic qualifications for a free place. But in 1837, John Bradley Dyne (1809-98) was appointed headmaster and during the next 36 years, ruling with arrogance and the rod, he transformed the place into a typical Victorian public school. One notable legacy is the Crawley Chapel, consecrated on Palm Sunday 1867, designed by F P Cockerell in red-brick Gothic. It was built in memory of George Abraham Crawley, a school governor.

In 2005 girls were admitted to the senior school for the first time. Ex-pupils of the school are referred to as 'Old Cholmeleians' as the school used to be known as Cholmeley School, after its founder.

Now take the pedestrian crossing over **HIGHGATE WEST HILL** to the **Gatehouse**. For centuries the parish boundary bisected the building, most of it lying in St Mary Hornsey, but the entrance from Highgate West Hill is built on an encroachment of Highgate Green and paid

poor rate to St Pancras from 1690. When its hall was used as a courtroom a rope divided the sessions to ensure that prisoners did not escape to another authority's area. Notice the parish boundary markers dated 1791 and the circular plaque recording the original gate house to the Bishop of London's park. Since 1994 the building has been wholly within the London Borough of Camden. The tavern was extensively modernised between 1891 and 1905. Earlier illustrations showed a plain Georgian building, part of which included staircase access to the passage over the archway ([3], p 22). This was demolished in 1769 for road widening. Tolls were abolished in 1876 and the gates were taken down in 1892.

Given its antiquity and importance for passing trade, the Gatehouse became a popular location for the strange Highgate custom of 'Swearing on the Horns', which is believed to date from the 17th century. The horns were the Forester's badge of office, and the custom may derive from an old admission ritual to a Fraternity of Drovers who travelled regularly to and from Smithfield and other London markets with their flocks. Latterly a device to boost beer sales and fleece unsuspecting travellers, it assumed cult status when Byron devoted a verse of *Childe Harold's Pilgrimage* to it, after himself being its victim. The ceremony consists of swearing a nonsensical oath, administered by

'Mine Host', before another who holds aloft a pole adorned with a pair of horns. At one time all 19 of Highgate's taverns indulged in the practice. In the days when all coaches passed the Gatehouse, it must have been very profitable for the publican. But after the opening of the Archway Road in 1813, many coaches transferred to the easier route. The custom died out as the railway took over from the coaches, but was revived at the Gatehouse in 1898. It is still re-enacted today, as a curiosity, at various local pubs, during the Mayor of Camden's 'Beating the Bounds' charity walk.

Turn left and pass **No.47**, Apothecary House, finely designed and rather more pretentious than its neighbours, with a pilastered and pedimented entrance and good cornice, built about 1730. From 1750 it was the home of medical families, notably generations of Wetherells, and was known as Wetherell House. The doctor and geologist Nathaniel Thomas Wetherell (1800-1875) lived here for many years. The next two houses adjoin each other and are set well back from the road, reached by their own driveway. The houses were built on the site of two cottages recorded before 1656. **No.46** was built in 1729, the date inscribed on its lead rainwater head, which also contains the initials of Joseph Davis, draper of Aldgate, and Eleanor his wife.

3 Drawing labelled 'Arch at Highgate'
(Wallis Bequest)

It, too, has a good porch. It is best known as the home of Grove House School, founded here by Zachariah Fenner in 1841, and continued 1885-1930 by Alfred Dickinson, and familiarly known as Fenner's. Francis Barraud, who designed the trademark for His Master's Voice, was sometime Art Master. **No.45**, also known as Ben Wyvist, was also part of Grove House School from 1885-89.

All three houses are on land enclosed in the 18th century from Highgate Green, which once stretched from here to South Grove ahead and as far east as the High Street. Their rear gardens abut the original boundary between St Pancras and Hornsey, and they stand at an angle to the modern roadway because they fronted a track which veered away from the Gatehouse to join Hampstead Lane. Heavily laden carts could use the track to avoid the archway, though not the toll.

Now turn to look at the terrace on the opposite side of the road. This part of the village, now part of Highgate West Hill, was known as Highgate Grove in 1800, and was later part of South Grove until 1939. The first building at the High Street end, housing a group of offices and shops at **Nos.49&50**, was built in 1850 as the Highgate District Police Station and Justice Room ('Y' Division). It closed in 1902. From 1912 it was a branch of Friern Manor Park Dairy. The terrace was built on wasteland enclosed by John

Leech, wheelwright, in 1692. **Nos.51-53** were erected in 1849. **No.54**, Pond House, with a tall mansard roof, probably dates from c.1739 but was refronted in the late 18th century. The Highgate Dispensary moved here in 1880 from Rock House, South Grove. The dispensary was founded in 1787 to provide medicines at cheap rates to the poor, funded by the subscription of wealthy residents, who could nominate needy persons for treatment. The National Insurance Act of 1911 made such dispensaries redundant, although subscriptions and donations for the Highgate Dispensary were still being recorded in 1928.

Alongside Pond House is smaller **No.55**, dating from the 19th century. This stands at the entrance to Pond Square (p 30), and attached to the first house in that street is diminutive **No.57**, Tadpole Cottage, dating from the mid-18th century. **No.58** provides an arched entrance to a yard. Here, in 1808, were the stables of Abraham Hale, coachmaster and "landau and fly owner". In 1823, his successor John Watkins was providing a daily coach service to London, with five journeys in the morning and four in the afternoon. The premises were rebuilt in 1881 in yellow brick with red banding and barge-boarded gables. In 1905, printers Hudson and Keane were here; Edward Hudson had founded *Country Life* in 1897. In 1940 the Ideal Laundry came and it was latterly the

offices of H W Cullum Detuners, leading experts in noise control. **No.59,** in the same style as No.58, replaced a house built in 1819 for John Long, a nurseryman. Nos.58&59 have recently been converted to residential accommodation.

Beyond the driveway on your right is the reservoir built by the New River Company in 1846, occupying a significant part of the old village green; the Company acquired the land in 1844. It supplied piped water to Highgate households (at least the rich ones) for the first time. The **reservoir** took the place of nursery gardens and the remains of one of the three village ponds. The railings and the circular "daintily stuccoed valvehouse" are original and Listed.

Opposite, Nos.60-63 form a rather ugly 5-storey Victorian terrace. Thomas Staniforth, the Principal of the Highgate Academy of Music, lived at **No.63** in 1884-87. This is followed by Nos.64-70, a more modest row, with mansard roofs and round-headed windows with 'Gothick' glazing bars. **No.65** was the headquarters of the Highgate Volunteer Rifles from 1901 to 1903, when it was exempted from rates, and **No.67** was the home from 1894 until 1920 of the bursar of Highgate School. At **No.70** Henry Wheeler had a timber yard in 1864, and next door, Edmund Kerry, another builder, operated 1914-27. The cobbled entrance to the yard survives. Small **Nos.72&73** were built in 1875 as

Victoria Cottages.

Pause at the end of the reservoir site, and beyond No.73 opposite is the **Flask**. A modern plaque suggests a date of 1665. Certainly there was a building here in 1663 on William Royles' "two pieces of waste", but the tavern was first known as the Flask in 1716. An oval tablet with the date 1767 and the letters WC commemorates William Carpenter, who then partially rebuilt the inn. During the 18th century, the Flask was used for St Pancras Vestry meetings as well as many sessions of the Cantelowes manor court. In 1975 "discreet additions" were made by E W Edwards. The inn is renowned as the location of the well-known sketch of a tavern brawl by the young William Hogarth.

Now turn right along a short road leading into **THE GROVE**. Turn right again and remain on the right-hand path. Beyond the railings enclosing the reservoir we come to inter-war **Old Well House**, a Neo-Georgian block of flats with two canted bays and big eaves. Continue to the last house on this side, Fitzroy Lodge (p 52), and note the boundary marks for Hornsey 1871 and St Pancras 1791.

Cross over the road and return along the west side. The first house is multi-faceted **No.12**. Designed by architects Lush and Lester in the 1970s for the Russian Trade Delegation, it replaces a house built on land sold by Lord Southampton in 1840. In 1864 it was the home of

Lt-Col. George Leach RE, then a Tithes Commissioner. John Bradley Dyne Jr, conveyancing counsel to the High Court and chairman of the governors of Highgate School, lived here from 1881 until 1909. The house was acquired by the Working Ladies Guild as a residential hostel in 1931.

Before the 1830s The Grove was a cul-de-sac of six late-17th-century houses (now Nos.1-6), first called the Long Walk, then Pemberton Row and by 1800 Quality Walk. It ended at the grounds of a house which stood on the site of No.12. This was the Grove House built in 1678 by judge Francis Pemberton upon the site of a yet earlier residence. That had been constructed by Richard Lyllie in 1610; leaseholder Thomas Collet built a causeway from it to the Chapel in 1662, presumably to avoid flooding from the pond. In 1733, Grove House was owned by the merchant Jacob Mendes da Costa. He was notorious for having brought (and lost) an action against his cousin Kitty in the ecclesiastical Court of Arches for breach of promise of marriage. He was the first Jew ever to do such a thing, and his application for the then astronomical sum of damages of £100,000 was dismissed. He published a partial and embittered account of the trial and is said to have been caricatured by Hogarth in the *Harlot's Progress* of 1732. A later resident was Charles Yorke (1722-1770), the Attorney General who accepted the post of Lord Chancellor only

to die three days later of extreme nervous tension. In 1782 the house and land were sold to Lt-Gen. Charles Fitzroy (1st Baron Southampton), owner of the land to the west. Soon after 1800 Grove House was demolished, although the Fitzroys retained its stables.

During the 1830s the Fitzroys decided to lease its grounds for building, which allowed The Grove to be extended into Hampstead Lane. The sites of Nos.10-12 were included in the sale of their property in 1840 (see p 52). Nos.10-11 are imposing mid-19th-century semis, with enormous bay windows. The resident of **No.11** in 1855 was the Rev. Charles Dalton, then vicar of St Michael's. It was later home to Annette Mills (1894-1955), the actor Sir John Mills' elder sister, who partnered *Muffin the Mule* in the children's TV show. Subsequently used as a hostel for overseas students, it became a single-family residence again in 1985. Next door at **No.10** John Lloyd, wine merchant and historian of Highgate, lived from 1902 to 1910. The house became St Michael's Vicarage in 1976.

We cross the top end of Fitzroy Park (p 52), and pass on the corner a strange building, sporting pilasters and a pediment. Once stables, it is now converted into a residence. The land here was formerly the "Great Garden" of Grove House and this site was leased for building by the 3rd Baron Southampton as early as 1831;

the transaction was recorded in 1836, by which time a detached villa had been built here. This is **No.9**, with its impressive Tuscan porch and delicate fanlight. The first ratepayer and occupant appears to have been George Smith, a wholesale farrier, who was here until 1855 when he sold the house to Edward Nettlefold, a wealthy screw manufacturer and one of the founders of the industrial conglomerate GKN (Guest, Keen and Nettlefolds). Nettlefold considerably enlarged the property, building what is now the separate No.9B, **Park House**, and adding the stables at the corner we have just passed. It is possible these enlargements were designed by his architect son-in-law, Thomas Chatfeild Clarke. During the 1930s residents of No.9 included the poet John Drinkwater and the wallpaper manufacturer Norman Shand Kydd (see also p 76). In 1955 **No.9A**, Westbury House, to the left, was erected by the architect and Fitzroy Park resident June Park; the rear is in a more contemporary design. In 2000 the upper floors of No.9 were rebuilt to return the house to something like its original appearance.

Nos.7A, 7&8 were built as a pair of semi-detached villas in 1833, after the Fitzroys had leased the site two years before. Note their first-floor iron balconies and original spear-headed railings. The librettist Christopher Hassall lived at No.8 from 1950 until 1953, when the actor Robert Donat moved in. Although not yet 50 he was by then a constant invalid and died five years later.

Having considered the 19th-century houses, we now turn to Nos.1-6 The Grove, the finest group of houses in Highgate. Dating from the 1680s they were built as three pairs of semi-detached houses, and are supposedly the oldest surviving semis in the London region. No.4 and No.6 are the best preserved.

The row of houses was a speculation by a City merchant, William Blake, to fund a 'Ladies Hospital' (a charity school) for 40 orphan children from London parishes. Blake's project remains a source of confusion and conjecture. His book, *Silver drops, or serious things*, published in 1680 as a form of public appeal for his venture, seems to have failed in its purpose. He acquired a "parcel of waste" on Highgate Green in 1679, and the houses were probably complete by 1681. He had also bought Dorchester House (p 69) and the Banqueting House, part of the Arundel House estate, a separate building where St Michael's church now stands, but had to sell the latter to his creditor Sir William Ashurst, who demolished it in the 1690s to build his grand new residence on the same site. Blake also owned another property which may have been the site of the Flask, which he was forced to sell in 1682, the year in which he was declared bankrupt and imprisoned. This resulted in severe mental

illness from which he never fully recovered. In 1683, Sir Francis Pemberton of Grove House, to whom he had mortgaged the six houses, acquired their freehold; the six houses known first as the Long Walk were subsequently called Pemberton Row. Pemberton also acquired Dorchester House, in which Blake hoped to resurrect his idea of the school in the mid-1680s; his *Humble Address to the Gentry of St Paul's, Covent Garden and St Giles* for subscriptions fell on deaf ears. In spite of accounts of a school with 36 pupils dressed in blue and yellow uniforms existing from 1666 to 1675, possibly in the adapted Banqueting House, it remains a mystery, and a sad end to a pioneering vision.

Parts of the garden walls of Dorchester House survive in the rear garden of **No.6**. The gateway to its front garden has a lamp overthrow, as have neighbouring houses. Lord Justice Sir Edward Fry lived at No.6 from 1864 to 1874, and his son Roger Fry, the artist and English champion of Cézanne, was born here in 1866. A later resident from 1916 to 1923 was the architect John Joass, designer of a number of large London shops including Mappin & Webb in Oxford Street and Whiteley's in Bayswater. More recently it was home for a decade until 2005 of the pop singer Annie Lennox, formerly of Eurythmics, living here with her second husband Uri Fruchtmann. She is one of a number of celebrities who have chosen The Grove as their London base.

No.5 was rebuilt by C H James in 1993, when fine wallpapers of c.1700 were discovered and transferred to the Victoria and Albert Museum. Although modern, it retains its original appearance. William Ford (p 92) was here in the 1850s and the stockbroker Alexander Scrimgeour (p 30) in the late 1860s. The Unitarian minister William Russell died here in 1871; in his youth he had been a painter but gave this up on being ordained. It was home in the 1930s to Sir Hubert Llewellyn Smith (1864-1945), described in the DNB as a "major architect of social and commercial policy of early 20th century Britain". He had contributed to Charles Booth's poverty survey in the 1880s and was Permanent Secretary to the Board of Trade from 1907 to 1919.

On the wall of the side extension to **No.4** note what appears to be an old fireback, featuring two men carrying a huge bunch of grapes. No.4 was home to the newspaper manager Sir Campbell Stuart until his death in 1972. He was a prolific, and extravagant, entertainer; at dinner parties here he brought together leading figures from the worlds of journalism, diplomacy, and business. **No.3**, which was altered by Seely & Paget in the 1930s, bears two plaques. The one at the top records the residence of Dr James Gillman who came here in 1823 with his lodger the poet Samuel Taylor Coleridge. Coleridge occupied a study bedroom in an attic with views overlooking Kenwood and here, at

6.30 am on the morning of 25 July 1834, he died. Coleridge received so many visitors that Dr Gillman organised his callers into regular Thursday evening soirées. D G Rossetti, John Stuart Mill, J Fenimore Cooper, Ralph Waldo Emerson, Thomas Hood, Harriett Martineau, Arthur Henry Hallam, Rev. Edward Irving and Leigh Hunt are but a few of those who toiled up the hill or walked across the Heath to see him, and, above all, to listen to him. Another, to whom Coleridge in his turn was able to pay his last respects, was Byron, whose funeral procession he watched as it passed the High Street in July 1824 on its way from Italy to Hucknall Torkard.

A later literary notable, as the brown plaque attests, was the author J B Priestley, who lived here for six years from 1933, when his *English Journey* was published. He wrote the classic comedy *When We Are Married* when living here with his wife, the archaeologist Jacquetta Hawkes. After WWII it was home to the businessman and public servant Sir Bernard Nathaniel Waley-Cohen, first Baronet (1914-91), the son of Sir Robert (p 57), and later to the merchant banker Sir Mark Cunliffe Turner, who helped form both Kleinwort Benson and Rio Tinto Zinc; he died here in 1980.

Francis Smith, a solicitor was at **No.2** between 1880 and 1900 and was responsible for planting the street trees in The Grove. Later residents were Yehudi Menuhin and his second wife, the ballerina

Diana Gould. They lived here from 1957 to 1981: Yehudi often gave violin recitals at nearby Witanhurst. At **No.1**, a Ladies' School flourished from 1891 to 1928. The school also encompassed the former neighbouring house Grove Bank (p 63) from 1895, and from 1900 No.2. The actress and theatre manager Gladys Cooper then lived here from 1929 until 1935 while married to Sir Arthur Neville Pearson and before leaving for Hollywood; she had Seely & Paget convert Nos.1&2 into one house.

Now it is time to leave the street. Descend the steps at the end of the gravel footpath, past the entrance to Witanhurst (p 68) and over the site of Dorchester House. Use the pedestrian crossing and turn left to reach the bus shelter in front of **South Grove House**. The present building is a block of 51 flats designed by Guy Morgan and opened in 1936. It was the demolition of the original South Grove House in 1934 by property developer Maurice Weston that led to the formation of the first Highgate Preservation Society. The site of the house was included in the Arundel House estate, and conveyed by Francis Blake to Andrew Campion in 1674. In 1720 Dr Henry Sacheverell came to live here. Sacheverell, a Tory High Church cleric, had been suspended in 1710 for preaching "bitterly" against the Revolution Settlement and the Act of Toleration. His sermon was burned by the public hangman, but Queen Anne presented him to the living of St Andrew,

Holborn, in 1713. Thomas Bromwich, a wealthy paper merchant, lived here 1759-88, giving his name to the ancient track Bromwich Walk (p 106), which ran at the edge of his property. In 1837, another famous Highgate figure arrived. Harry Chester was for 18 years assistant secretary to the Privy Council's Education Committee and was passionate about education for all. In 1839 he founded the Highgate Literary and Scientific Institution. With the Vicar, Rev. Thomas Causton, he transformed St Michael's School into an 'Industrial School', and was also involved in the campaign to prohibit Sunday trading in the village. After Harry Chester moved away, Angela Burdett-Coutts bought the house in 1857 to protect the northern boundary of her estate.

Continue ahead along **SOUTH GROVE** to pass on your right, No.18, **Voel House**. Dating from the 17th century, it was refaced in the 18th century when a top storey was added; its windows seem lost in its brick façade. Sir Hugh Owen, Permanent Under-Secretary to the Local Government Board, lived here from 1905 until his death in 1916; his educationalist father had been born at a farm called Y Foel on Anglesey and Sir Hugh gave No.18 its present name, from the Welsh for "brow of a hill". Outside Voel House is a tall milestone recording "IV miles from St Giles Pound". The inscription was changed from "V" to "IV"

by a local inhabitant who was affronted by its inaccuracy. Turn right, off the footway once known as Paradise Walk, and into the forecourt of **St Michael's** church.

The church is built on the site of Ashurst House, a grand seven-bay house with a pediment and cupola, constructed by Sir William Ashurst **[4]**, mercer and Lord Mayor of London in 1693, to replace the Banqueting House of Arundel House (see below). In 1724, Daniel Defoe was to write of it "a very beautiful house built by the late Sir William Ashurst on the very summit of the hill, and with a view from the very lowest windows over the whole vale, to the City; and that so eminently, that they see the very ships passing up and down the river for 12 or 15 miles below London". But the grandeur faded, and by 1816 the house is Daniel Dowling's 'Mansion House Academy for young gentlemen', a role it fulfilled until 1829. The owner, Sarah Cave, then sold it to the Commissioners for Building New Churches. Part of the terrace with its view over London survives, at the south end of the church.

St Michael's church, designed by Lewis Vulliamy (who later made Highgate his home) and built by William and Lewis Cubitt, was consecrated on 8 November 1832. It cost £8,171 (5 guineas per place) and provided 555 free and 1002 pewed seats. The thin stock-brick front and spire is similar to Vulliamy's now demolished

The Right Honble Sr William Ashhurst Knight LORD MAYOR of the CITY of LONDON. 1694

Christ Church, Woburn Square. The roof incorporates cast-iron trusses, and the wooden galleries are carried on iron beams. The aisle roofs have lost their pinnacles. Contemporary comment ranged from the euphoric: "it is impossible to imagine a more beautiful site than that chosen for the church, or a style of building better adapted to the situation", to the more guarded: "its style of architecture although not considered pure, is nevertheless, beautifully chaste". The nave and aisles were re-seated in 1878 and a chancel was added by C H M Mileham; the sanctuary was reordered by Temple Moore in 1903. In 1954, Evie Hone's last window, a brilliantly coloured Last Supper, was installed. The landmark spire was struck by lightning for the third time in 1903, and seriously damaged by blast from a flying bomb in 1944. Several monuments from the old Chapel were transferred here, including those to John Schoppens (1720), Sir Edward Gould (1728), Samuel and Mary Forster (1752 and 1744) and George Martin's tribute to Samuel Taylor Coleridge (1834). Coleridge was originally buried in the old Chapel. When this became ruinous, his remains, with those of his nephew Henry Nelson Coleridge, were transferred in 1842 to a vault in the old burial ground. This, in turn, became neglected. In 1961 the poet was reinterred under the aisle of St Michael's church, as a result of a campaign by the writer Ernest Raymond. In 1989, on the east side of the church, an imaginative Church Hall with memorial garden was built to a design by architect Melville Poole. A notice in the porch records that the floor is at the level of the cross atop the

dome of St Paul's Cathedral. St Michael's is the highest church in London.

As we return to South Grove, we have a good view of the backs of Voel House and – to our right, behind the 17th-century garden wall surviving from Ashurst House – **Old Hall**. Turn right to reach its front. Set behind high brick walls and impressive iron gates, it is a tall brown- and red-brick house of five bays. It was built in 1691 on the site of the southern part of Arundel House, the great mansion erected in 1588 by Sir William Cornwallis. Here he entertained Queen Elizabeth I in 1589, 1593, and 1594. The house was praised by Norden in 1593. Later, in 1604 it was the turn of James I to be entertained here with a performance of Ben Jonson's *Penates*. In 1610, the house passed to Thomas, 2nd Earl of Arundel. In between spells in the Tower, Arundel brought Wenceslaus Hollar, the artist and mapmaker, to London, and formed the first large art collection in England. It was to Arundel House, in 1626, that his friend Francis Bacon repaired after successfully refrigerating a chicken bought in Swain's Lane, with snow, before catching a chill. He died shortly afterwards. (Over the years, the ghost of this chicken has reputedly been heard squawking in Pond Square!)

The northern part of the mansion seems to have survived internally in its Tudor form, judging from the brochure produced by Mesdames Grignion and Hull, who ran a Ladies' Boarding School there from 1829 to

1846. In 1863 Old Hall became one house again when it was home to Sir William James Cotton, a City alderman who became Lord Mayor in 1875. After WWII the house was converted into flats; at No.6 lived the scientific instrument maker Robert Stuart Whipple. He was president of the Highgate Literary and Scientific Institution from 1937 until his death here in 1953. The house is now a single residence once more and during recent comprehensive restoration by architects Mark Reeves and Ian Bailey, structural evidence was discovered of the old Arundel House.

Opposite Old Hall are three one-storey 19th-century cottages, **Nos.23,24 & 25**, typical of so many in Highgate that have been destroyed. These buildings were empty for many years but are now in residential use and have been Listed Grade II.

BACON'S LANE, a private turning to the right just after Old Hall, leads to a small colony of seven architects' houses built in the 1950s and 1960s in the kitchen garden and around the trees of the former orchard of Old Hall. They were designed, among others, by the architects Sir Anthony Wakefield Cox, William Yuille and Leonard Manasseh for their own use. They take advantage of the view over London and the overgrown mystery of the cemetery below.

On the other side of **SOUTH GROVE** are the four modest red-brick houses of **St Michael's Terrace** dating from 1905. **No.22** is set back and has been recently reconstructed, while next door, **No.21** is a Victorian *cottage orné*, end-on to the street, with a surprisingly spacious garden.

On the far corner of Bacon's Lane on our right-hand side, we pass a former gardener's cottage and behind it a stable block, which both belong to Old Hall, whose owners used Reeves and Bailey again to restore the former and extend the latter. **Old Hall Coach House**, as it is now called, has a striking, sloping elevation with a prefabricated glazing system with rain screen cladding. Its design complements the neighbouring glass-fronted house at **No.16**. This was designed by Eldridge Smerin and was short-listed for the Stirling Prize in 2001; it won a RIBA Award in the same year and a Civic Trust Award the next. Its flat roof is topped by a dramatic glazed studio overlooking central London, and the windows have sophisticated, motorised roller blinds. Hearth Tax records in the 1670s record an earlier building here occupied by one Henry Plowman. The 1851 census records the building's name as Harcourt House, after General Harcourt (1743-1830), who distinguished himself in the American War of Independence, and who is known to have lived here. In 1869 it was completely rebuilt by Louis Pascal Casella, a scientific instrument maker, and called The Lawns. This was demolished, but its foundations were re-used for a house designed by the architect Leonard Manasseh in 1961, part of the group in Bacon's Lane; this was extended and enveloped by the glazed building we see today. The name 'The Lawns' survives on the gate posts; the far ones now have plaques recording the architectural awards given for the present house. Note the fine Victorian railings.

No.15, Bisham Court and previously Solsgirth House, was rebuilt in 1868. The original house of 1715 was a pair with Moreton House next door. In 1870, Rev. George Bartlett, a Congregational Minister, opened a school here which continued until 1896. No.14, **Moreton House**, was built in 1715 in the grounds of a mansion which is known to have existed at the top of Swain's Lane by 1580, when John Guilpin, a governor of Highgate School, was living there. In 1603 it was the home of Thomas Throckmorton, a prominent Roman Catholic. On 21 March 1602/3 he wrote to Sir Robert Cecil asking permission to remain at his house in Highgate for a time "for my urgent business about London". The first resident of Moreton House was Anthony Mendes, son of Catherine of Braganza's physician, Dr Fernando Mendes. Count Maltzan, the Prussian Ambassador, lived here in 1781, and from 1807 the physician Dr James Gillman with his young family. Nine years later, in the afternoon of 12 April, the poet Coleridge travelled up from Tottenham Court by the local coach to meet them, hoping that Gillman's medical supervision

5 Samuel Taylor Coleridge: pen-and-ink cartoon

S T Coleridge

would cure, or at least control, his drug addiction. Within three years Coleridge [5] had published many of his best known works, and had become Highgate's resident 'mentor and sage'. Thomas Carlyle wrote that "Coleridge sat on the brow of Highgate Hill in those years, looking down on London and its smoke-tumult, like a Sage escaped from the inanity of life's battle". Once again the village was to be a centre of pilgrimage. Thomas Gardner, organist and professor of music, made Moreton House his home from 1845 to 1873. In 1983 there was a serious fire, but the house was "immaculately reconstructed" over two years by Julian Harrap. Of five bays, the house has an Ionic wooden doorcase.

After the Restoration of the Monarchy in 1660, Highgate began to attract many nonconformist believers, probably because it lay just outside the five-mile limit (from the City) within which Dissenters were forbidden to preach. One Presbyterian with a licence to preach in 1672 was John Storer. He gave up his charge in Stowmarket and settled in Highgate, where he probably lived in a cottage on the site of nearby Church House (p 31). A Congregational Meeting commenced in 1834, and in 1859, under the energetic charge of Rev. Josiah Viney, the Union Church was built here to the designs of T Roger Smith. It had seats for 700, and large Sunday Schools were added later. After a period of disuse, it was revived in the 1980s for the **Highgate United Reformed Church**. With an Early-English-style stone front set back from the street, it remains true to its founders.

Turning, cross to the other side of South Grove, noting **Chesterfield Mansions** and **Burlington Mansions**. These red-brick mini-mansion flats with their exaggerated entrances were built for Arthur George Shearing in 1900. Although lacking the visual interest of the south side of the road, this area is of the greatest interest historically. All these houses stand on the former Bowling Green. In 1661 and 1672, the Lord of the Manor of Cantelowes gave ¾ acre of land to ten local residents in trust to safeguard the use it had had "since beyond the memory of man". Edmond Rolfe, the owner of the Flask, was granted custodianship in 1718. In 1730, perhaps because bowls was no longer fashionable, he was licensed to dig it up for seven years, provided that it would be restored to its former use two years after that. Unsurprisingly, it was not. A large house called Chesterfield Lodge was built on the site in 1806. From 1868 to 1870 this was home to William Longman of the family of publishers, and thereafter housed a succession of schools until 1895; it was demolished in 1899.

Burlington Mansions turn the corner into **POND SQUARE**, but today there is no trace of the ponds which gave it the name. Within this area, now surrounded by houses, but originally open and treeless, were two ponds, the product of centuries of sand and gravel extraction. As the village grew, so did the temptation to misuse the ponds. Water was illegally taken from them to water the roads and travelling cattle and many houses used them as cesspools, although they were the main source of drinking water, at least for the poor. On 28 May 1844, in reply to a deputation led by George Prickett, the local surveyor, the St Pancras Directors of the Poor ordered the two ponds to be drained. The parish fire engine was used to pump the water out, while farmers were allowed to remove the accumulated filth to enrich their fields. The western pond was filled in and paved over, and the other reduced in size and made circular and the road layout altered. By 1864, the remaining pond was a health hazard and was also filled in. Alexander Scrimgeour, a local stockbroker, suggested that a block of Model Dwellings be built in the square. A well attended and rowdy meeting was held at the Gatehouse, following which plans were prepared for Coleridge Buildings, which were built down on the Archway Road. Pond Square did not fare so well. There was a proposal to build a drill hall in it. Later, a fire station was built in 1894 by the St Pancras Vestry where the valuable public toilets now stand. Finally, with the help of a public subscription, it was possible to lay out formal planting and a children's playground. Today, the formality has, happily, disappeared, the trees have matured, and Pond Square has a character that is all its own. A registered 'town green', it now hosts open-air community events such as the annual Highgate Festival.

Beyond Burlington Mansions is **Rock House** and its 18th-century neighbours. Rock House, No.6, is the taller corner house with the two canted bay windows at first floor level. It is named after John Rock, merchant, and his wife Mary who lived here from 1841 until their death (and burial in Highgate Cemetery) in 1846. In the 1870s it served as the Highgate Dispensary. Of the other five houses behind Rock House, **Nos.1&2** have been partly reconstructed; the latter was home to the nursery gardener Eli Phippen before his move to Rose Villa (p 33). Nos.3,4&5 are in original form. **Nos.4&5** have broad-framed sashes; walls are of red brick with dark headers, and the mansard roofs are tiled. These houses stand on a piece of ground enclosed from Highgate Green in 1692 by Christopher Ryles.

Continue clockwise past the backs of the houses in Highgate West Hill, and turn right. By the ramp up to the Gatehouse stood an earlier fire station, built for Hornsey in 1814. **No.15** alongside the ramp was the home of the Menuhins from 1981 to 1983. It bears an unofficial blue plaque (of wood) to the canine Barking Lord Scruff of Highgate who lived here from 1985 until 1999, described as "music critic, dog poet, photographic model and all round good egg"; in summer this is obscured by creeper. No.15 is actually the back of a house in Highgate High Street (No.67), as are all the buildings on this east side of the square. Walk alongside them, past Listed **No.12**, refaced in Georgian style in 1893. Notice the difference in level between the square and the houses, especially at the lower entrance to the Prince of Wales pub (p 39), and observe, too, the recent balconies added to the houses at the eastern end.

At the bus stop, cross over to the Angel (p 38), which at present displays a plaster copy of the Winged Victory of Samothrace, and turn right along **SOUTH GROVE**. The first houses here were previously named Angel Row, being part of a single estate that also included the inn and two houses in the High Street. There is evidence of occupation on this site since 1489 and continuous records since 1610. At **No.2**, built by 1768, whose roof has been replaced by a penthouse, a grocery business was carried on for nearly a century. In 1901 Sam Billen began a 66-year service as a boot maker. The first recorded trader at **No.3** – in 1769 – was Rothwell, a coachbuilder. Taller **No.4** was bought in 1769 by the tenant Dolly Chandler, a baker, and a bakery it remained until recently; it is now a pizza restaurant. Nos.5,6&7 are a group of early-18th-century cottages with dormer windows, which were refronted and stuccoed early in the 19th century. They had long histories as butcher's shops. **No.5** retains its garden and is now residential, while **Nos.6&7** have been extended over the forecourt and now house a Café Rouge. The extension has a small tower with a clock and a weathervane. **No.8** was also refronted and stuccoed early in the 19th century and its garden built on for a shop. John Golden, the hairdresser here in 1824, was also the local organiser for the Society for Promoting Christian Knowledge.

No. 8 forms a pair with **Russell House** (No.9), built in the early 18th century. The latter was bought in 1760 by John Southcote. From 1799 to 1805 it was the home of Rev. Edward Porter, the first Congregational Minister, and his school. In 1876, William Marks, the Foreman of Highgate Cemetery lived here. Russell House has three relatively low storeys, three windows in width. The street front is of half-timber construction cemented over, with elaborate window frames and stucco decoration.

We now come to **Church House** (No.10), a large detached 3-storey house, Listed Grade II★, as are its gate and front railings. The site of No.10 and No.11 originally belonged to Sir Roger Cholmeley. There was at least one cottage here by 1610. The present house's first occupant was Peter Storer of the Inner Temple, in 1717. His son-in-law John Hawkins came into ownership in 1759. He was a surveyor and solicitor, Chairman of Middlesex Quarter Sessions in 1765, and was knighted. He then gave up his profession, devoting himself to music and literature.

He wrote a biography of Dr Johnson. His son John, in 1821, granted a 17-year lease of Church House to Hyman Hurwitz (1770-1844). Arriving in England in 1800, Hurwitz conducted a private academy for Jewish boys in Highgate, and became a close friend of Coleridge, who helped him obtain the professorship of Hebrew at the University of London. Leopold Neumegen continued the school until 1843 when it moved to Brighton. In 1858, the chief monumental mason in the village, Henry Daniel, came to Church House, staying for well over 60 years. Charles Henry Beck was living here with his parents in 1925, the year he joined the London Underground, for whom as Harry Beck he designed his famous Tube Map, topologically correct but topographically distorted.

Church House is one of the possible inspirations for 'Steerforth House' in *David Copperfield*. Dickens' description of the view towards the capital seems a little more realistic than Defoe's:

It was dusk when the stagecoach stopped with us at an old brick house at Highgate on the summit of the Hill. It was a genteel, old fashioned house, very quiet and orderly. From the windows of my room I saw all London lying in the distance like a great vapour, with here and there some lights twinkling through it.

No.10A, built as an annexe to Church House in 1848, is now used by the **Highgate Society**, as announced by the large sign above its one huge window. The society was founded in 1966 to "maintain the attractions, amenities and nature of the village" and is a successor to those who fought the developers in the 1930s. It runs a variety of activities for its more than 1,000 members but mainly concerns itself with planning issues, seeking to protect and enhance public amenities. It celebrated its first twenty years by planting a horse-chestnut tree, which stands on the traffic island by the South Grove bus stop. A plaque in the pavement there records that it was planted by Sir Yehudi Menuhin, then president of the society.

The Highgate Literary and Scientific Institution (HLSI) proudly proclaims its presence on the front of No.11. It was founded by the young Harry Chester "to promote the improvement of the mind by the cultivation of science and general literature in subservience to religion and morality", at a crowded meeting at the Gatehouse in 1839. The Institution moved to its present site in 1840 on St Pancras Day, 12 May. Initially it rented a collection of outbuildings, including two cottages of 1736, from the Jewish School then in possession of Church House. Today, the HLSI is a rare survivor of the quest for knowledge which blossomed in the aftermath of the Reform Act of 1832. Its survival, sometimes problematic, owes much to the devoted service of its officers, and to its Library which continues to meet a need in an area neglected by all three responsible local authorities. When finance (or the lack of it) threatened closure in 1874, it was only the discovery that the building lease could not be terminated for another seven years that gave a new secretary time to put the HLSI on a firmer footing. This was John Lloyd, who later published his *History of Highgate*. The building was rebuilt in 1879 by local architect Rawlinson Parkinson who added the Victoria Hall with its high timber roof and lantern, and converted the rear hall for the Library. Baroness Burdett-Coutts opened the new buildings with great ceremony in 1880. The porch was added two years later. Bomb damage in 1944 exacerbated another period of crisis for the HLSI but again it survived. In 1992 a full programme of renovation was undertaken. Today, its founder's intentions are maintained with a crowded programme of lectures, courses and exhibitions. Not surprisingly, it has been called "the heart of a London Village".

We have now reached the junction with Swain's Lane, marked by a collection of bollards. The conically shaped bollard nearest us is inscribed "St P/SWD/1855". On the opposite corner are red-brick **Nos.12,13&13A**. The present buildings date from 1888-94 when the cottage of John Fernee, cowkeeper in 1830, was rebuilt by Ernest Abbot for Charles Davies, the principal dairyman of the village. Some of his cattle grazed in a paddock behind his shop, but the main herd was on Parliament Hill. No.12 remained a dairy until 1982. Nos.13&13A are on the site of Ivy Cottage, first recorded in 1801, in possession of cowkeeper William Archer. Turn left into **SWAIN'S LANE**, taking care to avoid the traffic. Swain's Lane is first mentioned in the Cantelowes Court Rolls in 1481. It was mainly used as an access track to fields on either side. The first record of habitation was in 1609. By 1801 there were twelve cottages in an area called Swaine's Row.

At the top of the hill, on our left is Institution Cottage, at the rear of the HLSI. Built in the late 18th century as the gardener's cottage of Church House, it was used as sleeping quarters for the boys of the Jewish School, when that was based in Church House. It is now a private residence.

On the right is **Nightingale House** of 1993, built on the paddock attached to Charles Davies' Dairy. By 1951 the outbuildings here were shown as 'ruined'. A large storage building for H W Cullum Detuners stood on the site 1963-83. The Memorial Lychgate, entrance to No.107, was formerly the back door to the Sunday Schools of the Congregational (now United Reformed) church. It commemorates Highgate Camp members killed in WWI. Highgate Camp was started by the church

in 1907 as an annual youth camp. Its founder Jim Young was among the 14 (out of a total membership of 40) who did not return. Their names are on a plaque on the right hand side. A tablet on the left-hand side remembers Lt-Commander Dawbarn Young RNVR who was killed at Zeebrugge on St George's Day 1918. The camps continued until 1938, using a field at Aldwick (near Bognor), by which time there was a membership of 140.

Continue to a private roadway on the right, along which were built **Nos.91-103**, a stylish 3-storey terrace by Haxworth and Kasabov (1970-72), with living rooms on the top floor. No.95 was the home of the civil servant and author Sir Alan Neale, who died here in 1995; he had been Permanent Secretary at the Ministry of Agriculture when Britain joined the Common Market. Just beyond is the disused north entrance to Highgate Cemetery (p 14), its gates securely locked. Peer through them and to the left you will see a minute, cement-faced lodge and on the right wall two green slate memorials, one to the architect Anthony Wakefield Cox (1915-93), who designed his own house at nearby No.5 Bacon's Lane.

The yellow-brick terrace was built on the site of Rose Nurseries started by Eli Phippen, whose house **Rose Villa** can be seen opposite (at the entrance to Bisham Gardens), with its date 1880 recorded. Cross over to it. Looking back towards

South Grove, we cannot avoid the eyesore of Highgate, the garages and technical clutter for the **BBC Telecommunications Mast**, whose antennae have shared the skyline with the spire of St Michael's church since 1939 when the original 150-ft-high timber structure was erected. The site had been acquired by the BBC in 1937 for receiving and transmitting radio and television signals. Television outside broadcasts required radio links but the receiving aerial on top of the Alexandra Palace had proved unsatisfactory as it was de-sensitised by the proximity of the television transmitter there. So the Swain's Lane mast relayed TV broadcasts to Ally Pally until the outbreak of war when television was suspended and it started to broadcast the BBC's new wartime radio services, the Light Programme and the Home Service. During the war, however, the Swain's Lane site became a listening post capable of monitoring the sound signals from German aircraft. It could activate the Alexandra Palace transmitters by remote control, to jam radio reception by German aircraft. This resulted in only one-fifth of German air raids getting through. It resumed its more mundane role after the war. Today, it is used as a radio mast for London Taxis. Is it impossible to tidy up this corner?

We now turn into **BISHAM GARDENS**, which was named from former Bisham House. Records of Bisham

House go back to 1553 when Richard Hodges, a founder governor of Highgate School, is recorded in possession. In 1688, the house was owned by the Gould family (Edward Gould, merchant and his wife Elizabeth). In 1818, Captain Peter Heywood retired here. He had been a 16-year-old midshipman on HMS Bounty and got left behind when Captain Bligh was set adrift. As a result, when he returned to England he was tried for mutiny. He was eventually freed and resumed his naval career. Promoted to captain in 1803, he became a distinguished hydrographic surveyor. Heywood moved to Regent's Park in 1829, but returned to Highgate to be buried in the old Chapel in 1831. As recorded in contemporary illustrations [6], Bisham House was a sizeable, comfortable-looking Tudor house of 2½ storeys, set

back from the High Street with an ample driveway. It was demolished in 1884.

No.23, opposite, beyond the Telecommunications Mast and with a railed roof terrace, was converted into a residential property only in 1930 when the ground behind ceased to be used as a stonemason's yard. The other houses in Bisham Gardens were designed by John Malcolm and built by Alfred Imber, who lived at **No.21** with his family. This house was built in 1885 and the street was completed in 1892. No.21, appropriately, has special tiles in the porch. The Imber family finally moved away from Highgate in 1986 and W A Imber recalled the time in the 1930s when the Imbers were repairing St Michael's spire, and he, as a boy, would climb to the top on a clear day and sit admiring the unobstructed view down the Thames to Tilbury (so perhaps Defoe's description was not so far wrong).

Bisham Gardens provided much-needed accommodation for middle-class families in the centre of the village. **No.9** and **No.11** were both homes to Francis Cunningham Woods, head of music and organist at Highgate School from 1901 to 1930. The headmaster of St Michael's School and Librarian of the HLSI, John Parker Wilson, died at No.11 in 1935. Walter K Jealous, the *Ham and High*

6 'Captain Heywood's Cottage', alias Bisham House (P Heywood, 1827)

editor, who lived at **No.7** in 1901, also wrote *Reminiscences of Highgate 1860-1902*. On the right-hand side, **No.32** was the home of Margot Jefferys (1916-1999), the first professor of medical sociology at the University of London. The barrister Francis Russell Burrow died at **No.28** in 1945. He was a keen tennis player, wrote many books on the subject and was the tennis correspondent of *The Observer*. Charles Ackland, the first Vicar of St Anne's Church, Highgate (p 83), retired to **No.22** in 1900 where he died 10 years later, and Miss Emille Ruhig ran a school at **No.14** from 1908 until 1921.

At the end of Bisham Gardens, we reach **HIGHGATE HIGH STREET**. By the 18th century, Highgate had the makings and appearance of a small town. The High Street, with its predominantly 17th- to 19th-century houses and shops, contains few architectural masterpieces, but the general massing and roofscape as the brick terraces rise to the crown of the hill is very satisfying, and few recent intrusions spoil the restrained mixture of colours and materials used. On the Camden side there was little scope for the expansion of commercial premises. On the northern (Haringey) side, by contrast, the properties are very deep, giving space for numerous courtyards and backland development.

Turn right past the Highgate Bookshop at **No.9**. When built in 1887, in connection with the formation of Bisham Gardens,

these tall 4-storey buildings with shops (Nos.3-9) were called Nos.1-4 The Promenade. Before becoming a bookshop, No.9 was a grocery, as well as being the Post Office from 1913 to 1921, a service which has been provided since then by **No.7**. It is interesting that Highgate village never seems to have had a purpose-built Post Office. Beyond No.3 is the entrance to Waterlow Park.

At this point the walker may choose to enter Waterlow Park and take in the circular Route 2.

Otherwise, cross by the lights to the opposite (Haringey) side where the High Street begins just above Cholmeley Park. The present buildings of **No.2** (Elgin House) and **No.4** date from c.1805, although they are considerably altered and now house a restaurant. No.2 was a boarding house for Highgate School 1851-1884. The auctioneer George Prickett was at No.4 in 1830. His creation, the firm Prickett and Ellis, returned in 1899 and stayed until 1967. Martin Motors used both buildings in the 1940s. Nos.6&8 is a modern office building, **Stanhope House**, of 1987, a successful addition to the street, with good massing and details. It replaced two houses dating from 1813. From 1899, both were used by the Highgate Steep Grade Tramway Company (p 46) as offices, engine house and depot until the line was closed. In 1911, R Martin's Garage began

its long association with the High Street here. Stuccoed **No.10**, The White House, was built in 1705 and was the Nag's Head from 1719-65. Next to it is **Parkview Mansions**, a solid block of red brick flats with excessive dormers, pillared porch and good ironwork. This replaced two houses demolished in 1907. These were No.12, Oxford House, built in 1809 for Robert Harding, linen draper and No.14, Hornsey House, in which John Atkinson lived in 1813 and John Holme the phrenologist in 1829, and which later housed the London and South Western Bank.

At No.16 is the **Duke's Head**, which has featured in licensing records since 1781. The mock Tudor front of the present building is disappointing. Enter **Duke's Head Yard** to see Tayler & Green's **Studio House**, built for the artist Roger Pettiward in 1939. It has a miniature tower with rooftop terrace, a seminal Modernist design, which was much publicised. Beyond is **Duke's Point**, a modern enclave of brick-built houses.

Back in the High Street, **No.18** was initially built c.1825 and at the start of Queen Victoria's reign housed Richard Crump, brushmaker and undertaker. Charlotte Bishop, stationer was here from 1918 until 1947. During her tenancy there was a fire after which the house was reconstructed, in 1921.

Without crossing the street, observe the houses on the Camden side. Beyond

Bisham Gardens, **Nos.11,13&15** were all built in 1887 as part of the development of the Bisham Gardens estate. The houses beyond are Listed Grade II*. **Nos.17,19&21** were part of Lady (Elizabeth) Gould's Charity estate. Elizabeth was the wife of Edward Gould; she died in 1691 and her Trust took effect upon her husband's death in 1728. There was a house here on the High Street in 1636. By 1667 it was "three messuages". In 1728 the houses were placed in the care of three trustees appointed by the vicar of St Pancras "for the benefit of the poor inhabitants of the town and vill of Highgate". In 1733, Robert Harrison built the present houses, which have raised ground floors and segment-headed windows, hooded entrance doors and tiled roofs with flat-topped dormers. **No.23**, Englefield House is the best in the street. It was built by 1710, and conveyed by Edward Gould to William Pilton of Piccadilly, wireworker. Of brick, it has straight-headed windows and fine rubbed-brick lintels; inside there is an original staircase and wall panelling. This house has been the home of medical families since 1892.

Continue up the Haringey side, considering Nos.20-40. Nos.20&22 were probably built in 1821 by the builder Thomas Broadbent, on an estate of 3½ acres along this side of the High Street that was left to Christ's Hospital in Jane Savage's will dated 1669. The hospital sold the pair in 1922. In 1876 No.20 was called

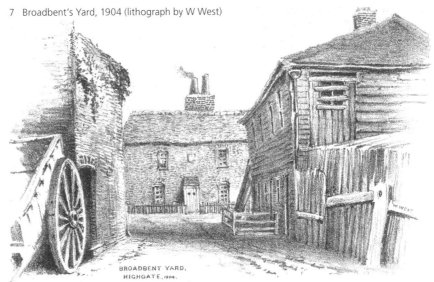

7 Broadbent's Yard, 1904 (lithograph by W West)

BROADBENT YARD, HIGHGATE, 1904.

Commerce House and was occupied by Mrs Bryce, a fancy draper. **BROADBENT CLOSE** (formerly Broadbent's Yard **[7]**) was developed from 1920 for Martin's Garage. This toothless gap now too clearly reveals the mess behind.

In **HIGHGATE HIGH STREET** the house at **No.24** was built as No.1 Feary's Row in 1794, as a wall plaque attests. Samuel Feary was a shoemaker at No.35 on the opposite side, in 1769. Nos.18-22 and Feary's Row (Nos.24-40) present an unusual line of late-18th or early-19th-

century roofs and upper windows when seen from a distance farther down the Hill. At **No.26**, John Golden, a hairdresser, plied his scissors from 1825 to 1873. At his funeral, local shops closed as a mark of respect. An early trader next door at **No.28**, in 1813, was Susannah Boston, a whitesmith, while her neighbour at **No.30** kept a stationer's shop. The first recorded tradesman at **No.32**, a linen draper and silk mercer, was followed by Prickett & Venables, who combined auctioneering with a sideline in wines and spirits. In

1918, the firm of William Cutbush, nursery gardeners (p 70), came here. The property had been amalgamated in 1841 with **No.34**, where the first recorded occupant was Miss Thorne, straw-hat maker. **No.36** was Miss Gladys Constant's milliner's and dressmaker's from 1911 to 1967. At **No.38**, in 1851, John Osborne combined the craft of silversmith with the making of umbrellas, while at **No.40** in 1873 we find Herbert Sigismund Koch, professor of languages.

Now it is time to look again at the Camden side of the street. Note the raised pavement to protect pedestrians from street filth in the days when many drovers passed through Highgate. **No.25**, next door to Englefield House, dates from c.1780. Stanley, one of the Attkins family of butchers, was a poulterer and fishmonger here from 1907 to 1954, followed by the butchers W R Mudd until 1984. The Highgate firm of Prickett and Ellis Underhill now at **No.27** (Granville Cottage), was founded in 1767 by John Prickett. His grandson Frederick published *Antiquities of Highgate* in 1842.

A short history of the Prickett family and firm in Highgate is in order here. In 1767 John Prickett, a carpenter, held a property auction in Highgate Village. On his death in 1789 his son, also named John, continues the business of auctioneer and surveyor, and in 1831 the firm becomes John Prickett & Son, the son being George (b.1796), who was to have seven children.

In 1880 Frederick Venables joined to form a short-lived Prickett & Venables, and in 1885 the name became the familiar Prickett & Ellis, with the formation of a more successful partnership with Henry Ellis. Between 1920 and 1930 the business expanded to three offices – Mr Prickett's original Village office at No.32 (moving in the 1930s to No.4 Highgate High Street), Henry Ellis's Archway Road office, and a new commercial department under Henry Ellis the younger in Chancery Lane (bombed in WWII and never reopened). With the redevelopment of No.4 in the 1960s Tony Ellis moved the Highgate office to No.27, where it remains to this day. In 2000 Christopher Underhill took over the Highgate Village office, which now trades as Prickett & Ellis Underhill.

Nos.29-33 are recorded in 1783. The builder Thomas Broadbent operated from **No.31** from 1858 to 1875. An archway next to it is marked Highgate Health Centre, a homeopathic clinic which operates from the rear of **No.31A**. The archway leads to **Bullens Yard**, named after the 19th-century local coal merchant and grocer John Bullen. At the end of the yard stands **No.29**, a 4-storey 18th-century house.

At early-18th-century **No.33** we come to the Angel Row estate. By 1610, the site of Nos.33&35 contained a row of cottages, standing back from the road, in the ownership of William Steere, citizen and

skinner of London. No.33 was in the same ownership as The Angel (p 38) until 1876. **No.35** was, in 1769, two houses occupied by the shoemaker Samuel Feary.

We have now reached **TOWNSEND YARD**, known as Prickett's Yard until the 1850s. It leads into the extensive backland today occupied by the Highgate Garden Centre. Exploring this would involve a foray deep into Haringey territory, but it is worth a quick walk down to the entrance of the Garden Centre for the extensive view north-eastwards towards Epping Forest. The land on these slopes has long been used for nurseries; Highgate Cemetery had a nursery here from 1904 to 1960. On returning note to the left, beyond the row of garages, an isolated cottage **No.36A** with steep mansard roofs. It is the remnant of a row of similar cottages built behind the High Street.

By 1890, Townsend Yard had become a 'blackspot'. It contained a large number of picturesque but unsanitary timber cottages. The Hornsey Local Board demolished those nearest to the High Street, but the ones further back survived until 1934. A thatched cottage at the bottom end of the lane, the home of Jack Foster, Highgate's last water carrier who died in 1855 aged 79, was still being used as a store in the 1940s by Samuel Andrews, market gardener. And then there were the pigs. The Attkins family had 70 or 80 sties at the end of the yard in 1860.

The present house at the corner of

HIGHGATE HIGH STREET at **No.42** was occupied by James Townshend *[sic]*, builder, in 1813 and the yard was his place of business. The house was another of the properties of the Christ's Hospital estate that was sold in 1915. The door hood shelters the Ashurst coat of arms, which was brought here when Ashurst House was demolished in 1831. There is another coat of arms, that of the City of London, on a small lead plaque at first-floor level. This is presumably an old fire insurance mark; there is an identical one, painted gold, on No.62. **No.44** on the opposite corner of the yard was the chemist's shop run by Thomas Henry Dunn, with its convenient side entrance. It was patronised by Coleridge during his years in the village. Dunn's prescription books from 1813 have survived, with details of many of his clients. Dunn's young assistant Seymour Porter, son of the Minister of the Independent Chapel, became used to Coleridge's visits to the 'back shop' via the side door. Dr Gillman's regime seems never to have completely cured Coleridge of his addiction. He would consume a wineglass of laudanum a day, replenishing his flat half-pint bottle every five days. Porter, on his afternoon off, would track Coleridge to his favourite walk in Millfield Lane to listen and learn from the poet.

Nos.46&48 are a wooden-framed pair of cottages with a brick front. **No.46** has an 18th-century doorcase. It was a baker's for over a century from 1837, run for most of that time by the Freeman family, who moved to Crouch End in the 1920s and still continue in business there. It has been a bookshop since 1938. The Coopers Arms occupied **No.48** between 1765 and 1902, by which time the demand for beerhouses was on the decline, and it became a health food store for over 50 years. At **No.50**, an early-19th-century building, Charles Saunders' chemist's shop was another half-century survivor, from 1899 to 1949, while at **No.52** the Penrose Electrical Company served the village from 1934 to 1984. No.52 was rebuilt in Queen Anne style, with red-brick and stone banding, in 1895. At the same time **Nos.54&56**, now painted white overall, were also rebuilt in a similar, if grander, style, by Trueman and Watson for the London and South Western Bank. This became part of Barclays in 1916, and Barclays Bank is still here. George Prickett, surveyor, is recorded at No.56 by 1823.

Cross the road by the lights to **The Angel**, first recorded as the "Cornerhous" *[sic]* in the Cantelowes record for 1489. John Wyking, who then occupied it, was the village aletaster, so it may not have been an inn while he lived there. His landlord Giles Eustace did brew ale, and in 1524 he leased a brewery, on the site of the Angel, to John Dery, which contained "two leads, a horsemill, utensils, vessels and other necessaries belonging to the said brewery". The inn existed by 1610. In 1663 it was occupied by William Fisher, whose name appears on a trade token of 1669, the first known use of the name 'Angel' for this tavern. The timber-framed inn was rebuilt in 1880, and the rather severe frontage to the High Street was created in 1928-30. Behind it runs **ANGEL YARD**, the inn's stableyard which still has granite setts, but its stables with hay lofts have been converted to residential use.

Look back across **HIGHGATE HIGH STREET** to No. 58, which has the distinction of once housing Marriott's, Highgate's last corn chandler, which closed in 1950. In fact, it seems always to have dealt in corn. George Kent, who was here in 1853, gave his name to **Kent's Yard** behind. **No.60** has an interesting white-painted, weather-boarded exterior with a surviving hoist, reminding us that this, too, was a baker's and corn chandler's in the 19th century. **No. 62**, another Christ's Hospital property, retains its external canopy, betraying its use until 1916 as a butcher's shop, which is made clear from the modern inscription. The canopy kept the sun from the meat. Even if it is no longer a butcher's, there is a good advertisement for Palethorpe's sausages on the side wall.

The story of **Nos.64&66** is somewhat complicated. The houses stand on the site of the White Lion inn. This was a 1730 conversion from an older house and became, for a while, the most prominent

8 Undated drawing, 'Highgate Village, showing the High Street, Dodd's Smithy and Pond Square from the Angel Inn'

Highgate, from the Angel Inn

tavern in the village for assemblies, balls and public meetings. It was also used as a theatre in the mid-1820s, when Harriot Coutts (p 102) was patronising actors there. The building was demolished in 1831, and Nos.64&66 were built. In 1832 Thomas Dunn, chemist, moved from No.44 and began to make soda water on the premises; in 1977 the old soda water vat was found *in situ*. The shop front was replaced in 1864, inserted between the doorcase and carriage arch of the former inn. No.64 remained a chemist's until 1967 and is now once again a pharmacy.

On the Camden side there is now a large gap north of the Angel, beyond the entrance to South Grove: No.39 and No.41 are missing. No.41 was the site of the village blacksmith [8].

Thomas Sconce worked his forge here in 1664. Later, the Dodd family carried on the business for 150 years. The Forge, an antiquated building with a tree growing through the roof, was demolished in 1895 and rebuilt as a printer's. This too was removed in 1939, a victim of the march of progress. Trams (see p 46) had presented no problems at their High Street terminus; they just reversed over a pair of points onto the other track. Trolleybuses, and their successors, needed turning space, which is

why No.41 had to go.

It stood at the southern end of the row of buildings that separate Pond Square from the High Street, erected on "the bank before the Elms" on which the first cottage had been built in 1619. Nos.47,49& 51 stand on this site today. Cross over South Grove to reach them. The whole row was referred to as Watch House Row in 1796. The name York Place was later used until

officially abolished in 1893. At **No.47** Geoffrey and Anne Lewis ran a florist's from 1931 to 1987 and at **No.49** in 1889 George Shorter established dining rooms which lasted until 1950. Lloyds Bank has been at **No.51** since 1929.

Beyond is the **Prince of Wales**, an early-18th-century building refronted in the 20th and a beerhouse since 1864. A century later, Leslie Compton was in charge. He had been an Arsenal and England footballer and Middlesex cricketer, just like his more famous brother Denis. Next door, at **No.55**, which was rebuilt in 1893 with much terracotta decoration, we meet the Attkins family again. In about 1832, James Attkins left the employment of Samuel Attkins at No.82, and set up shop here. The business lasted until 1968. At **No.57**, in 1935, Alex Wylie started a bakery shop which traded until 1986.

Traffic permitting, we can now look across to the Haringey side and consider the remaining houses and shops. Nos.68-82 are a range of low, plain 18th-century houses, mostly refaced and converted into shops but with roofs and window lines adding to the uniform character of the street. At **No.70** in 1894 were the printers May & Co. and the office of the *Hampstead and Highgate Express*. The present newsagents Brooksby maintain a tradition going back to 1918. At **No.72**, in 1837, George Potter, the London antiquarian was born. His father was a bootmaker. George went to a dame school run by Miss Moore in Broadbent's Yard. He later made his money in wholesale bootmaking. He retired early, devoted himself to public affairs in the village, and at his death in 1927 left 29 volumes of London information and a further extra-illustrated copy of Prickett's *Antiquities of Highgate* to the British Museum's Department of Printed Books (now part of the British Library). Potter

also commissioned postcards with prettified scenes of old and contemporary Highgate by the artist William West. At **No.76** in 1802 was Richard Dermott, a perfumer, and next door in 1813, Thomas Keeble, gardener and greengrocer. **No.82** has another canopied shop front from which we can guess that it was once a butcher's – trading originally as Samuel Attkins, father and son, and then under other names until 1977. Note the charming bow window above the entrance to its yard. Here there was a row of pens, once used for veal calves, which were converted into gallery space by the Centaur Gallery that occupied No.82 from 1960 until 1999. The gallery was run by the painter and sculptor Jan Wieliczko and his wife. They specialised in displaying work by Polish artists.

No.84 has a good 19th-century shop front. In 1947, H E Frolic was repairing wireless sets here. The **Rose and Crown**, with another 19th-century front, was licensed by 1730. It was the base from which regular patrols escorted evening travellers down to Islington in the later 18th century. In 1842 it provided a dinner of boiled beef and plum pudding to some of the 30 men and 100 boys 'Beating the Bounds' of Hornsey parish. "Ethiopian Entertainers" were engaged in 1860 to encourage beer sales. **Nos.88&90** have been rebuilt in recent times, albeit in an 18th-century style, but No.88 has been a grocery shop since 1799, when James

Poulter is recorded. The local firm of Walton, Hassell and Port were here from 1965 until 1987. No.90 was part of No.88 until 1888. Six years later it became a coal merchant's office, run by the local firm of Thomas Lea & Sons. They were taken over in 1920 by Charringtons, who stayed here until 1952. This building turns the corner into Southwood Lane, which has a particularly fine collection of old houses facing Highgate School, but these are all in Haringey.

Returning our attention to the Camden side, the houses get smaller and narrower until we reach the corner with Highgate West Hill. **Nos.59&61** were rebuilt for offices of the Hornsey Local Board before becoming estate agents Sturt and Tivendale in 1918, and later Day Morris. At the north end of the row was the watch house and cage, built when Highgate obtained its Lighting and Watching Act in 1774. The architect William Inwood surveyed the cage in 1820 and reported it to be 7ft x 7ft x 6ft high with no openings whatever. He thought it could contain 5 or 6 people huddled together. Despite these shortcomings, the possession of these instruments of civil order proved that Highgate was not only physically but socially head and shoulders above its neighbours.

The walk is completed,
and the Gatehouse beckons.

Waterlow Park and Highgate Hill

Circular walk from the upper (Highgate High Street) entrance to Waterlow Park

For modern map see back cover

On this circular route through Waterlow Park and up Highgate Hill we take in the sites of several large houses, in which key figures in Highgate's history once lived, and get the chance to see several others that are still extant. The walk begins in Highgate Hill at the upper (Highgate High Street) entrance to **Waterlow Park**, which can be reached by buses to the 'Bisham Gardens' stop.

This access to the park was made possible by the demolition of a large property called Hertford House. By 1664, there were two houses on the site. They were combined in 1705, and then rebuilt during Dr Bernard Snow's occupation (1816-40) by Lewis Vulliamy, who was later to live in Cholmeley Lodge across Highgate Hill. From 1850 the house was in the possession of William Hickson, wholesale shoemaker in Smithfield, who had profited from supplying boots to the Army during the Napoleonic wars. His youngest daughter Anna-Maria had married Sydney Waterlow in 1845. His eldest son William Edward Hickson bought

and edited the radical *Westminster Review*, having published his best-selling *The Singing Master* in 1836. William Edward coined the aphorism "If at first you don't succeed, try, try again" and also wrote a third verse to the National Anthem.

Hertford House was included in the estate that Sydney Waterlow presented to the London County Council (LCC) in 1889, and was demolished in that year. On the left-hand side of the park entrance, behind a high wall, is **Fairseat**. This house stands on the site of Sir Roger Cholmeley's Tudor residence, which in 1802 was bought by William Bloxham, a Lombard Street stationer, in whose family it would remain for nearly two centuries. In 1856 it was leased by Alderman Sir Sydney Waterlow (1822-1906), printer and Lord Mayor of London, and given its present name, after his father-in-law's house named Fairseat, near Wrotham, Kent. In 1867, the house was comprehensively rebuilt in high Victorian style in white brick, with steep French mansard roofs and patterned slates. The lease was due to expire on Lady Day 1925. Sydney Waterlow repeatedly tried to persuade the Bloxhams to sell the reversion of the lease, always without success. In 1865, however, he had bought the freehold of the large neighbouring estate of Lauderdale House (p 47). In 1879 he wrote to Lord Rosebery that "to assist in providing 'gardens for the gardenless', and as an expression of attachment to

the great city in which I have worked for fifty-three years, I desire to present to the Council, as a free gift, my entire interest in the estate at Highgate". This free gift was enthusiastically accepted at a crowded meeting of the LCC on 12 November 1889, and the Council, with the help of its architect Thomas Blashill, set about preparing the estate for its new function. Sydney Waterlow had hoped that Fairseat might become a museum, but this the Bloxham family would not allow.

In 1909, to the Bloxhams' fury, the LCC decided to widen the High Street to allow a double track for the new electric tramway which was replacing the former cable system. This entailed demolition of the east wing of Fairseat, and the house was refronted in red brick. In 1926, a fresh lease was granted not to the LCC but to Channing School. Fairseat became the Junior School, which it has remained to this day except for a short interval during WWII when the school was evacuated to Ross-on-Wye; the house was then used briefly as a British Restaurant, catering for those involved in Civil Defence.

Until 1995, the main feature of the upper entrance to Waterlow Park was a magnificent cedar of Lebanon, a survivor of the Hertford House garden. Unfortunately, it had rotted inside and after 200 years it had to be felled.

Proceed downhill along the main path lined with benches. At the fork in the path bear left (in WWII a flying bomb landed near the tennis courts to the right, near the air raid shelters constructed beside them). We now have a long view over London. Glancing at the Nature Conservation Area with a pond (Upper Pond) fringed by a board walk on the right, turn sharp left and walk for 150 metres to a statue honouring the founder of the park. Sir Sydney holds a key, symbolic of his gift of a "garden for the gardenless", and he carries a furled umbrella, which makes the statue unique in London. It cost over £500, and was unveiled by HRH Princess Louise, Duchess of Argyll, on 28 July 1900. The sculptor was Frank Taubman. There are plenty of benches here on which to sit and take in the view, and consider the history of Elm Court, a house which once lay close to the site of the statue.

We know that Widow Sell had a house here in 1582, but the Highgate historian John Lloyd considered that Elm Court grew out of outbuildings attached to Lauderdale House. Surviving illustrations show a comfortable 2-storey L-shaped house with parts obviously built at different times. This house was recorded as a 'tenement' in 1756; by 1801 it was a 'mansion'. From 1828 to 1839 it was used as a school. Dr Benjamin Duncan moved his Commercial Academy here in 1828 from The Bank (p 49). His advanced views were shared by his chief language teacher, Joachim de Prati, a follower of Saint Simon

and a former colleague of Pestalozzi. Dr Duncan offered an adventurous curriculum of practical subjects including astronomy, biology, chemistry, architecture, surveying, logic and elocution. There was no corporal punishment, fagging, competition – nor holidays, since he held that "vacations were very prejudicial to the interests of young gentlemen". This meant that unlike other boarding schools he made no extra charge for boys from the colonies. His school lasted only three years at Elm Court; it was followed by William Addison's boarding school, which stayed for eight.

The last occupant of the house was also the most famous. Sir James Pennethorne (1801-1871) was a distinguished architect and town planner who had studied under the elder Pugin and was principal assistant to John Nash. He designed Victoria and Battersea Parks and was responsible for many of the major London street improvements. He came to Elm Court in 1842, three years after his appointment as architect and surveyor to the Commissioners of Metropolitan Improvements. During his tenancy the house was often called Elms Court.

Retrace your steps to the main path and walk down to the 'Lime Avenue'. Only one side of the tall limes has survived, but new ones have been planted recently as replacements. This was once the carriage drive from Swain's Lane that Pennethorne created to serve Elm Court in preference

to the steep and less private approach from Highgate Hill. When Pennethorne left Highgate in 1864, Sydney Waterlow demolished Elm Court and adapted the drive to serve Fairseat. Follow the avenue past the shelter on the right, and on the left note the circular asphalted area where a wooden, thatched bandstand once stood; band concerts here were very popular. The octagonal bandstand fell victim to arson in the 1960s, as did its rectangular replacement two decades later. In both World Wars the park, like other open spaces across London, was used for allotments in which people were encouraged to grow their own food; in WWII, sheep and cattle were also kept in the park. The land was recovered for park land only in the 1960s, when the remaining fruit trees from Pennethorne's 1860 orchard were grubbed up.

The pathway downhill now curves to the right to meet **SWAIN'S LANE**. At the gate, Pennethorne built a delightful lodge (1849), now ochre-painted, with an excessive number of Tudor-style chimneys. Pause here. Farther up the hill on the left side of the road there once lay a group of modest cottages known in 1801 as Swaine's Row, and, in 1834, South Hill Cottages. The adventurous may wish to ascend the very steep section of the road to reach their site. The first cottage was recorded in 1609, and the 1801 map shows twelve dwellings, including one larger property that has been identified as the house of

Dr Elisha Coysh. A painting claiming to represent it **[9]** shows a substantial twin-gabled house, timber-framed and plastered, but oddly enough on a level site. Coysh was a physician with special skill in treating the victims of plague. He was living here from 1657 until his death 29 years later (his grandson, a wine cooper, remained until 1751). In 1659, Dr Coysh had been licensed to lay three yards of water pipe from "Swines Well in Swines Lane" to his house. Plague sufferers would have found Swain's Lane a suitably obscure route to allow them to escape from the City unnoticed, and especially attractive if medical treatment was also available.

After the cemetery was laid out in 1839, most of the cottages were used by gardeners, gravediggers, monumental masons and sextons working there. There were also greenhouses here until nurseries were purchased in Townsend Yard (p 37) in 1904. A watercolour of 1906 shows old 3-storey houses. As the cemetery declined, so did the cottages; by 1939 only one was inhabited and this was damaged beyond repair in 1944. During the 1950s the derelict site was used as a builder's yard and by two firms of toolmakers. The first of three substantial houses, **No.89**, appeared in 1955, followed by **No.87** in 1966 and **No.85** in 1978-82. No.85 was designed by John Winter, but its blue steel developed structural problems and it was recently demolished. A replacement, the

9 'The house once the residence of the Celebrated Plague Doctor Coysh as it appeared in 1720', from a drawing … copied by W Burden, 1802

'Deconstructed House' by Eldridge Smerin architects, with large areas of glazing capitalising on its close proximity to the cemetery, was under construction in 2007.

From outside the lodge we now examine, across the road, Stephen Geary's "thin brick Gothic" gateway (1838-9) to **Highgate Cemetery** (see p 14). The plaster rib-vaulted arch leads into a carriage courtyard, with protected shelter for mourners. It is flanked by two former mortuary chapels: the Anglican chapel to the left is now a museum/exhibition area; the former Dissenters' chapel to the right was gutted in 1975 and has been converted to offices.

Walk further down Swain's Lane to the entrance to the Eastern Cemetery. Pause here and look across the road. Behind a high wall, smothered in ivy, is **No.82**, a pioneering house of 1966-69 by John Winter. It is framed by Cor-ten steel, which has weathered to a rust finish in harmony with the woodland character of the surroundings. It won a structural steel award; the steel (made with copper) is said to be good for 800 years, which should make it last longer than Winter's other house in Swain's Lane (p 43). No.82 was built in the grounds of the adjacent **St James Villa**, at the southern edge of the cemetery. Erected in 1880, with decorative bargeboards, it was the official residence of the Cemetery Superintendent, Frederick Tabois, a Huguenot who had lost his lands in Belgium. He lived here for 25 years, his daughter marrying the headmaster of Grove House School. In 1905, shortly before he died, he moved to what is now No.45 Highgate West Hill.

Returning to **Waterlow Park**, admire the splendid iron gates, recently restored. Go back around the curve of Lime Avenue and, before it begins its rise towards the central shelter, turn right along the path towards the large green dome in the distance. The path crosses a bridge which soon after WWI replaced the original 'rustic' bridge between the Middle and Lower Ponds, connected by a cascade. The Lower Pond was created in 1893 when the park was formed, although there had been a pond here in earlier times, filled in by 1763. The Middle Pond to your left has had a continuous existence since at least 1582, when it was mentioned in a deed of sale. In the 19th century its use was shared by the residents of Lauderdale House and Elm Court. Both ponds are man-made and fed by springs at the top of the park.

Beyond the bridge take the right fork, which leads past the new **Park Centre** (2005). From 2003 to 2005 great improvements were carried out to the park – the largest in Camden – with the help of Lottery funding (Heritage Lottery Fund Urban Park Programme) at a cost of some £1½ million. Below, to our right, is the lower kitchen garden, part of the formal gardens of Lauderdale House, which we visit later.

Leaving Waterlow Park at the Dartmouth Park Lodge Gate, turn left. Opposite is the austere west face of **St Joseph's Retreat** (accessed from Highgate Hill), which was opened by Cardinal Manning in 1876 to house a community of then mostly Italian-speaking priests and monks. Modelled on a rustic Italian villa, the Retreat was designed by F W Tasker to harmonise with the first incarnation of the adjacent St Joseph's Catholic church. Note the statue of a young priest, under a stone canopy at the corner, and in the garden a very large statue of St Joseph.

Passing another entrance to Waterlow Park (St Joseph's Church Gate), ascend to the junction with **HIGHGATE HILL**. Before traffic lights were installed at this complex junction, it was known locally as Suicide Corner. Here the three boroughs of Camden, Haringey and Islington meet, successors to the parishes of St Pancras, Hornsey and Islington. Two parish boundary stones are set into the pavement; the Islington one, dating from 1741, is illegible now, but the date of 1794 can be made out on that of St Pancras. At this point there was also once a tollbooth.

Looming over us is **St Joseph's** church – in Islington, but impossible to ignore. The green dome of "Holy Joe's" is a prominent landmark that is visible for miles. This, the mother house of the Passionists in England, is one of the large Catholic churches (St Dominic's Gospel Oak is another) built on prominent sites around London after the re-establishment of the Roman Catholic hierarchy in 1850. It covers the site of the Old Black Dog tavern, which once stood on this corner. Thought to have been trading by 1552, it was disused as a pub by 1826. In 1858 the Passionist order was in search of a permanent English headquarters, which had to be outside London but close enough to serve it. When the Black Dog was advertised for sale, the Passionists who came to view the property did so disguised as laymen, for fear of the local prejudice against Papists. Just nine years earlier, locals had rioted when Father Ivers had rented a room at No.17 High Street to celebrate mass. The pub and surrounding land were sold for £4,500 at auction, conveniently for the Brothers, who thus had no need to reveal their identity in advance.

The Passionists were led by the autocratic Father Ignatius. He was a brother of the 4th Earl Spencer. A former Anglican priest, his life's ambition was to reconvert England to Catholicism.

Rehabilitated for religious use, the pub was dedicated by Cardinal Wiseman on 21 October 1858. The purpose-built chapel, a modest affair by E W Pugin, was completed in 1861. Two decades later an original congregation of 30 had grown to 2,000, swollen by an influx of Irish navvies into Upper Holloway. A temporary iron church was erected in the grounds while a larger replacement church was built. The present Italian Romanesque building, designed in 1887 by Albert Vicars, was erected to celebrate Pope Leo XIII's Jubilee. The restrictions of the site dictated the plan, the lantern atop the dome illuminating the sanctuary with its elaborate baldachin. The new church was blessed by the Bishop of Liverpool on 21 November 1889; week-long celebrations ensued, during which huge crowds came from far and wide to see the interior.

Cross over carefully at the traffic lights into the forecourt of the church. Its front has plenty of statuary, including Saints Peter and Paul, and high up, a crowned Madonna and Child. Below this, above a doorway is a roundel depicting Pope Leo XIII. Facing the church is a painted crucifixion shrine, which incorporates a WWI memorial.

Now look across to the other side of Highgate Hill (also in Islington). Here is the **Old Crown**, a gin palace of 1898 with conical roof, on the corner of Hornsey Lane. To the left, between that road and Cromwell Avenue (both in Haringey), stands the former Presbyterian Church, built in 1887 by the architects Potts Sulman and Hennings. Of Kentish ragstone, it has a prominent tower and spire in the Decorated style. The porch of 1900 is by G Lethbridge. The church was closed in 1980 and converted into flats (**Cloisters Court**).

The houses across Cromwell Avenue from the church and higher up Highgate Hill are on the site of a large house, Winchester Hall, which was demolished in 1881. The first building on this site was constructed for Robert and Anne Smith. Robert was the fifth son of Thomas 'Customer' Smith (1522-1591), a prominent figure in the City and Collector of Customs and Dues in the Port of London. Anne Smith's son John let the house to the goldsmith Sir John Wollaston (1585/6-1658), who became Lord Mayor and purchased the manor of Hornsey. A godly puritan, with John Ireton he sewed up Highgate for the Parliamentary cause. After the Restoration, the house reverted to relatives of the Smith family. It was occupied by a widow called Susanna Winch, and throughout the 18th century the house was known as "the Winches house". The Tudor house had been taken down by 1691, and an equally large replacement built. In 1801 the Commandant of the Highgate Volunteers, Nathaniel Harden, was here. The furrier Peter Poland subsequently owned the house; his son Sir Harry Bodkin Poland, born in 1829, became a well-known barrister. The silk mercer Giles Redmayne (cf. p 84) moved here in 1838, the family staying until 1853. Eight years later Winchester Hall became the home until 1874 of Lt-Col William Jeakes (of the Bloomsbury Volunteer Rifles), inventive ironmonger and Highgate benefactor. His son sold the house in 1881 to the Imperial Property Company who demolished it, auctioning the fittings including 1½ miles of iron railings. Photographs show a bulky brick house of 3 storeys with a recessed centre and pedimented doorcase.

Re-cross Dartmouth Park Hill with care to the corner of Waterlow Park, on the Camden side of Highgate Hill. This road was built in the 14th century as an alternative route out of London to the North and Scotland. The citizens of Islington and St Pancras were by 1380 granted 'pavage' funding to maintain the road from the foot of the hill, although the route through Highgate and the Bishop of London's park was probably open by 1318. The earliest use of the name dates from 1565, but was usually applied to Highgate West Hill, Highgate Hill itself being more commonly called Holloway Hill. It became a turnpike under the Islington Act of 1717, and is shown as 'Holloway Road' on Thompson's parish map of 1796. The name Highgate Hill was consistently applied to this road only from the mid-19th century.

Over the years, the road surface had become deeply rutted by coaches and wagons and especially by 'cattle on the hoof', and drastic action had to be taken to protect the property lines along the edge of the road. After fresh thunderstorms the "hill would become smooth again as the waters removed the wheel and hoof ruts" (taking the road surfacing with it). And the gradient was formidable. Pepys recorded, on his visit to Lord Lauderdale, that "six horses were put into Lord Brounker's coach" i.e. two more than usual.

In the later 19th century horse-drawn trams were being introduced all over London, but they were never an option for the steep slope of Highgate Hill. Instead, a cable tramway was introduced, using the principles of the San Francisco system. The Highgate Steep Grade Tramway was the first of its kind in Europe. It was a narrow-gauge line (3½ ft). Andrew Smith Hallidie (1836-1900) had invented the patent cable-grip that was used, and his assistant W Epplesheimer was the site engineer here. He had received the endorsement of Sir Sydney Waterlow who had seen the cable cars in America and who claimed, somewhat optimistically, that "the machinery is very simple…rarely if ever out of order".

The line was opened on 29 May 1884 and ran from Archway Tavern (the terminus for several horse-drawn tram lines) to Highgate Village [10]. The Engine House was at No.8 High Street, and the wheel pits at the head of the line were outside Nos.55 and 82, under the roadway. Trams towed trucks up the hill with coal for the engines and with other heavy goods. In 1892 the line closed because of poor maintenance, brake failures and worn-out cables. It reopened in 1897 in time for Queen Victoria's Diamond Jubilee. In 1899 a descending car went out of control, both driver and conductor being drunk. In 1908 the London County Council bought the line for £13,000. It closed on 23 August 1909.

It was then rebuilt with double standard-gauge tracks and reopened 7 months later. The new line, designed by A N Coles, cost £17,452, and necessitated the removal of Fairseat's east wing. Class 'M' trams with special slotted brakes were used initially, being replaced in 1931 by the LCC's special HR/2s, twin bogie cars for steep grades. As no overhead current collection was involved, no trolley poles were fitted.

The service now ran to Moorgate. On 9 December 1939, the last tram left Highgate, and the next day trolleybus route 611 started, a year later than planned because of objections to overhead wiring in the village. The J3 and L1 trolleybuses were fitted with 'runback' brakes. In their turn, the trolleybuses were phased out, the last leaving the terminus in South Grove in July 1960. Routemasters on route 271 took over. In November 1965, double-decker 'Atlanteans' were introduced as an experiment, the first one-man-operated front-entrance buses to run in London.

On the opposite (Haringey) side of Highgate Hill are Nos.92-102, a tall red-brick, late Victorian terrace, built to appear like semi-detached pairs. They were constructed in 1882 on the site of Winchester Hall and had concrete foundations. **No.92** was the home of Norman Thomas Carr Sargant, a once wealthy metal broker, who died here in 1946. The Sargant family had a long association with Highgate and in the 19th century were living in Trays Hill House on nearby Hornsey Lane. Norman's children included William Walters Sargant (1907-88), who became a noted psychiatrist after himself being admitted to a mental hospital. He was a fervent advocate of the physical treatment of mental illness. His brother Tom (1905-88) set up the law-reform organisation Justice and was its first Secretary for 25 years. Tom's daughter Naomi (1933-2006), also a Highgate resident, was Professor of Applied Social Research at the Open University and a pioneer of lifelong learning. **No.98** bears the name Mount Melleray, after the Trappist monastery in Ireland.

On the Camden side, we walk alongside an old brick wall, parts of which may date back to the 17th century. Attached to it is a drinking fountain of the Metropolitan Drinking Fountain & Cattle Trough Association. The cattle trough, probably once very welcome to horses toiling up the hill, has long gone.

A little farther up, turn left to enter the forecourt of **Lauderdale House**. To the side and rear of the house enjoy the restored lower garden and the upper terrace, with its historic walls and eagles, and a large sundial, enclosed in a railed circle with a quotation from a poem by Andrew Marvell. Then visit the café or enter the house.

Among the few survivors of its kind in London, albeit with many later additions and alterations, Lauderdale House is basically a late-16th-century timber-framed house on brick foundations, its external walls now covered with pebbledash. There is an early brick basement beneath the entrance hall, and vaulting under the courtyard. The veranda with its Doric colonnade is c.1780.

The house dates from c.1580 when Richard Martin, a City goldsmith, lived here. He was Master of Queen Elizabeth's Mint and a supporter of Francis Drake, the Protestant privateer. One of his sons was among the first colonists of England's first lasting settlement in North America, Virginia. By 1599 the estate included a garden and 15 acres of land. Sir William Bond enlarged the estate with land along

10   The Highgate Steep Grade Tramway:
car no.10 in the High Street

Highgate Hill and Dartmouth Park Hill, which enabled terraced gardens to be developed in the 17th century. In 1610, Lady Arabella Stuart, cousin of James I and a potential successor to the throne, stayed here on her way to detention at Barnet. In 1641, Mary, widow of the 1st Earl of Home, bought the house. At her death in 1644 she left two daughters, Margaret and Anne, wife of John Maitland, the 2nd Earl of Lauderdale. A foul and unprincipled Royalist, he was imprisoned in the Tower of London for nine years until the Restoration. In the meantime, John Ireton, puritan MP for London, Lord Mayor and governor of Highgate School and brother of Cromwell's general, occupied the house. Lauderdale, "a bold and unabashed liar", returned in 1660. Under Charles II he became virtual ruler of Scotland and was made a Duke. Tradition has it that he allowed Charles' mistress Nell Gwynne to stay here and receive the king. As recently as 1993, research uncovered fresh evidence to substantiate this familiar story.

Lauderdale had left by 1677, when it was sold to William Mead, patron of the Quakers, whose founder George Fox recorded his visits here at the time. Mead's acquittal, with William Penn, the founder of Pennsylvania, at the Old Bailey of charges of unlawful assembly established the principle of a jury's independence in reaching a verdict. Mead was one of a succession of merchants who enjoyed the

11 'Croquet at the Convalescent Home of St Bartholomew's Hospital', Lauderdale House (*Illustrated London News*, 27 Sep 1873)

place. One of the first (and the last owner-occupier), Sir William Pritchard, a Tory Lord Mayor of London in the 1680s, left a lasting mark. He had earned his fortune supplying bricks for the building of forts along the Thames and it is likely that the massive, recently restored, garden walls came from the same source. Merchants gave way in 1794 to a Ladies' School run by Mesdames Kearton and Sheldon.

Other schools followed. In 1837 Thomas Howe took over and carried out extensive alterations. James Yates arrived in 1848 and the house regained its place as a venue for scientific and literary discussion. Besides being a Unitarian Minister and scholar, Yates was also an enthusiast for rare plants. He constructed a pioneering octagonal palm house, which unfortunately the LCC demolished in 1889. Yates died here in May 1871. Sir Sydney Waterlow had bought Lauderdale House and its grounds in 1865, and after Yates died he leased the house in 1872 to St Bartholomew's Hospital as a convalescent home [11]. In 1878, the St Pancras Guardians of the Poor, against the wishes of the Vestry, attempted to buy it as a site for a new workhouse. The Hospital moved out in 1885, and in 1889 it became part of Waterlow's gift to the LCC. Initially the Council resolved to demolish it but, deprived by the Bloxhams of the use of Fairseat and in face of massive protests led by William Morris, they restored it in 1893, creating five flats for park keepers. Further repairs were undertaken in 1961 and again in 1963 after a fire. It has been owned since 1971 by Camden Council, which has leased it to the Lauderdale House Society as a Community Arts Centre. Partially restored, it was reopened by Sir Yehudi Menuhin in October 1978.

Return now to Highgate Hill and look at the houses opposite on **THE BANK**, the road raised above the main Hill,

emphasising the extent to which centuries of feet, hooves and wheels have beaten the ground down. The houses are numbered as part of **HIGHGATE HILL**.

At No.104 **Cromwell House** is the largest surviving 17th-century house in Highgate, and is Grade I Listed. It was built c.1638 by Sir Richard Sprignell, a Trained Bands Captain, replacing an earlier house recorded in 1605. It has 2 storeys with basement and dormers, and is seven bays in width. Built in red brick with much rubbed brick decoration, John Summerson called it "a tour de force on the part of some bricklayer contractor". The interior has a fine ornamental staircase, original panelling and ornamental plaster ceilings. Externally, the extra bay over the carriageway to the right was added in 1678 during the ownership of the da Costa family, who became the first Jews to own landed property in England since medieval times. A rich merchant, Alvaro da Costa, acquired the house in 1675. He had come to England from his native Portugal shortly after the Restoration and had reputedly been a page-boy of Catherine of Braganza. He lived here with his family and cousins, one of the rooms being used as a private synagogue. The family connection ended when his grandson Abraham sold the house in 1749. From 1834 to 1842 it was a gentlemen's boarding school run by William Addison. After Addison left, Rev. Gerard van de Linde ran the Collège Français

until 1859, and was followed by Rev. Henry Stretton until 1867. The roof and cupola were restored after a fire in 1865. In 1868, the house was taken on a long lease by the Hospital for Sick Children as a convalescent home. In 1924 it became the Mothercraft Training Centre, and in 1953 the Zenana Missionary Society arrived. In 1970 the Monfort Missionaries moved in and stayed until 1983. Then followed some years during which the fabric was at serious risk from developers (in spite of its Listed status). In 1987 it was converted into offices by Carden and Godfrey who carefully restored the interior and added a large extension to the east on the footings of a wing built by the da Costa family. In November 1990, Cromwell House was sold to the Ghana High Commission for use as an embassy, and it is their flag that flies outside, celebrating (in 2007) fifty years as an independent nation.

Next door, at No.106, **Ireton House** is named not after Cromwell's general but after William Ireton, its owner in 1895-1905. It was built as one house with Lyndale House (No.108) around 1725 on the site of an older structure. Emma Williamson ran a Ladies' School here from 1884 to 1894. **Lyndale House** acquired its name in 1895. Nos.106&108 are both Listed Grade II★. Of roughly the same age **No.110**, Margaret House, also has Tuscan pilasters, but its third storey and attic have been rebuilt. Smaller **No.112**, The Cottage, was first built as an addition to Margaret House.

Continue walking up the Hill, noticing the stone in the left-hand wall, opposite No.112. It records the entrance to the house which was known as 'Andrew Marvell's Cottage' **[12]**, and which was demolished in 1868 as part of Sydney Waterlow's improvements. The first reference to a house here is a tenure pre-dating 1582 in the name of a Richard Dickens. The same house was occupied by George Prior, a London merchant, in 1662. Illustrations show a 2-storey cottage of ancient appearance. No documentary evidence has been found to justify the tradition that Andrew Marvell actually lived here. Marvell was born in 1621. According to his letters he did live in Highgate in 1675 when George Prior was in occupation. From 1657 Marvell was an associate of Milton and Dryden in the Latin Secretaryship. He was elected MP for Hull in 1659. He was a poet of gardens and nature, but also the author of scathing political satire and radical scourge of Royalists in particular. He wrote this of his ostensible next-door neighbour in Highgate, the Duke of Lauderdale:

> *The Scotch-Scalado of our Court, two isles*
> *False Lauderdale, with ordure, all defiles.*

Marvell died suddenly in 1678, of poison or apoplexy.

Look again at the row of tall buildings on The Bank. The large block known as

Haigh House was built in 1954 over the site of a pair of late Georgian semi-detached villas that were damaged by a landmine in 1940 and subsequently demolished. Former No.116 was named Arundel House in the 1880s, as it was then believed by historians (including John Lloyd) that this had been the site of that mansion (cf. p 28). However, there had been a different large 16th-century house here, occupied

50

in the 1650s by Sir John Wollaston, Lord Mayor of London. Another Lord Mayor, Sir Thomas Abney, who died in 1722, is reputed to have been a later resident, and the great hymn writer Isaac Watts was a frequent visitor for over 30 years. A remaining wing survived until 1828, and drawings show a curious, but unmistakably Tudor, 3-layer design. Here was the Highgate Commercial Academy run by Dr Benjamin Duncan from 1813 until 1827, before its move to Elm Court (p 42). In the 1890s 'Arundel House' was the home until his death in 1899 of the Unitarian Minister Rev. Robert Spears, who helped to found the Channing School, which took over this house in 1930, having occupied the adjoining Hampden House at former No.118 in 1925.

The next two houses form a pair, of the same design as the former Nos.116&118 and dating from 1829. No.120, **Slingley**, was occupied in 1871 by Robert Carr and first called Slingley House. Robert Carr was a blacking manufacturer, and the great-grandfather of the Robert Carr who was Home Secretary in 1972. No.120 was absorbed into Channing School in 1921. Its neighbour No.122, **West View**, was leased in 1886 by the school, which purchased it in 1901.

The last house on The Bank is No.124, **Sutherland House**. This formidable late-19th-century building replaced a house that was here from about 1800. It was a boarding school in 1802 and was home to no fewer than five schools in succession before becoming the pioneer building for Channing School in 1885. It was rebuilt in 1899. **Channing School** was founded by Miss Matilda Sharpe, Miss Emily Sharpe and Rev. Robert Spears for the daughters of Unitarian Ministers. The school is named after William Ellery Channing, a prominent American Unitarian, who had visited Highgate in 1822. Matilda Sharpe was billed as 'Manager' in contemporary directories, a task at which she must have excelled as within 50 years the school had taken over most of The Bank, in addition to Fairseat. Further buildings were added to the main site during the 20th century, including assembly halls in 1927 and 1962, and science buildings in 1983.

Beyond the road called Cholmeley Park are the 1930s flats of **Cholmeley Lodge**. They cover the site of the Mermaid Inn, which was the oldest recorded building on this site, dating from 1619, when George Ray sold it to William Priestly. It had 10 hearths and survived as an inn until 1679. It was demolished in 1776. In that year, the original Cholmeley Lodge was built, set well back from road, by Charles Causton. The architect Lewis Vulliamy lived here between 1851 and 1853. This house was demolished in 1931, although its lodge – the miniature white-painted building with a patterned slate roof – survives opposite. The present flats, designed by Guy Morgan, were completed in 1934. They have a dramatic curved front of 6 storeys, with alternating brick and white rendered bands, a design which aroused much opposition, but which is extremely successful and very well maintained. They are Listed Grade II★. Barbara Castle MP lived here in the early 1960s at a time when she frequently sued for libel; in 1961 she lost her action against Chris Chattaway MP, who had taken exception to her claims that British soldiers were torturing people in Cyprus.

On the Camden side we pass Fairseat. Opposite, **No.128** and **No.130** are a pair of 3-bay brick houses with straight-headed windows and a heavy cornice, built about 1700. Both are Listed Grade II★. At Ivy House (No.128) in 1829 lived George Crawshay, the ironmaster who gave St Michael's its clock and bell. Later residents included Charles Knight, the author and publisher of the *Penny Cyclopaedia*, and from 1895 A C Irwin, the father of the novelist Margaret Irwin. At Northgate House next door, Miss Parrish ran a preparatory school from 1829 to 1833.

We have now come full circle and regained the upper entrance to Waterlow Park.

Around Fitzroy Park

Circular walk from the Gatehouse (including a section of Hampstead Heath; wear suitable shoes)
For modern map see back cover

This route explores an area that was once the core of a 100-acre estate that belonged to the Fitzroy family, the Barons Southampton. They secured the freehold of the Manor of Tottenhall or Tottenham in 1768. This northern portion of the manor was its demesne land, which stretched as far south as the River Fleet at the foot of present-day Highgate West Hill. The Fitzroys lived until 1810 in a house they built here, then leased it to various tenants until 1825, after which it was pulled down. The absentee landlord Charles, 3rd Baron Southampton, finally decided in 1840 to sell the estate for building. The prospectus for the sale (11 August) stated that 50 elegant villas with gardens had already been built, as well as several mansions in Lord Southampton's park demised to "merchants and professional men of the highest character and respectability". The rest of the land was parcelled up into 1-2 acre plots, on each of which the sale map rather hopefully shows a detached villa. Few of these materialised; indeed, 28 lots were withdrawn and sold privately to Lord Mansfield, who wished to protect the fringes of his Kenwood estate which lay to the west. Development of Fitzroy Park was sporadic after the sale and although now quite built up, mainly with large 20th-century houses, it retains a distinctly rural air, abutting as it does on Hampstead Heath and being extensively wooded.

Our walk starts at the Gatehouse (p 20). Turn the corner left into **HAMPSTEAD LANE** and take the pedestrian crossing to reach the north side. This offers a better view of the south (Camden) side, on which we shall focus. Hampstead Lane was originally an early medieval track at the edge of the Bishop of London's park in Hornsey, forming the parish boundary with St Pancras. A toll was levied on travellers both at the Gatehouse and at the Spaniards Inn at the other end. The road was known as Cane Wood Lane by the time of Queen Anne, and Caen Wood Lane by 1774, gaining its present name in the early 19th century. In the 1790s Lord Southampton and Lord Mansfield persuaded the Bishop of London to divert the road some yards farther north, away from their properties. The new route lay north of the parish boundary, and Hampstead Lane was wholly in Hornsey, later the London Borough of Haringey, until 1 April 1994 when the south side of the road was assigned to Camden.

There were no houses at the Highgate end of Hampstead Lane until the 1830s. The track had formed the northern boundary of Highgate Green until houses were built there in the 17th century. These buildings faced south towards Highgate village. Off Hampstead Lane were stables and coach-houses for the Gatehouse, which were sold off in the late 1880s; **No.1**, a large gabled building, was afterwards constructed on the site. Behind the big oriel window on the first floor is the hall of the theatre known as **Upstairs at the Gatehouse**, which opened on 12 December 1997 with 128 seats. The hall was built in 1895 as "a place suitable for Balls, Cinderellas and Concerts", and in its time has been used variously as a music hall, a cinema and a Masonic Lodge. In the 1960s it was the venue for a jazz and folk club at which Paul Simon (of Simon and Garfunkel) once appeared. In the 1970s it lay derelict, and from this period dates the story that it is haunted.

At **No.3** in 1921 the long-established Highgate auctioneer's firm of Prickett & Ellis (see p 37) opened a furniture sales room, here during the interwar period. One of their first sales was the state coach of Baroness Burdett-Coutts. Three Bells House at **No.3B** is set back, a modern affair of sloping roofs, built in 1967-68 by S & M Craig for themselves. It adjoins 1830s **Fitzroy Lodge**, built on the site of the Fitzroys' stables and initially owned by the coachmaster Abraham Hale (p 23). It is a Grade-II-Listed, stuccoed building with broad eaves and stands on the corner of The Grove (p 24), of which it forms a part. It is now split up into flats, but in the 1850s was home to the City bookseller Eneas Dawson, and in the 1870s and 1880s to Rev. Robert Leslie Morris, a master at Highgate School, who taught pupils here. On the side wall of the house, in The Grove, are parish markers (see p 23), testimony to the original course of Hampstead Lane.

Cross North Grove and continue, noting opposite at the next corner **No.5**, a tall detached house built in the late 1850s of stock brick, recently cleaned. Nos.7-15 beyond form a terrace that was built in the grounds of No.5 from 1870 and then numbered Nos.1-5 Hampstead Lane. Nos.9-11 bear the name Grove Lodge. **No.7** (formerly No.1) was home to Talbot Baines Reed (1852–93), managing director of the family typefounding business Sir Charles Reed & Sons Ltd, and a children's writer. His books for boys, mainly school stories, aimed to provide wholesome reading and appeared first in serialised form. Reed died here of consumption, aged 41. **No.13** (then No.4) was home in 1871 to the architect John Wimperis, and in the 1880s to the writer and local historian John Sime, who died in 1904. The house was occupied by the Australian artist of religious and symbolic imagery Arthur Merric Boyd (1920–99) from when he first came to London with his family in 1959.

Cross over Highgate Close, built in the 1960s on the site of St Michael's vicarage.

The modern houses beyond on the north side lie over the entrance to the Highgate Cottage Gardens that were opened in March 1847 by Harry Chester (p 27) to encourage labouring men to cultivate allotments. It was never a success and closed in 1899 when Highgate School needed land for playing fields.

Opposite, **Nos.17&19** are a 'Tudorbethan' pair with very pointed gables, first erected as Fitzroy Park Villas. **No.21**, set back behind tall conifer trees, is an imposing stuccoed house built as Park Villa in 1842 by Thomas Lea, a wealthy coal merchant. Lea would drive to London in his phaeton with two loaded pistols which he left at the Duke of St Albans pub at the foot of West Hill and collected on his way home. Fear of highway robbery still existed into Queen Victoria's reign. Park Villa was held by the Lea family until 1902 and its grounds, like those of the adjoining houses, stretched south to Fitzroy Park until houses were built along that road during WWI (although No.21 still retains a rear entrance there). In the 1990s No.21 was home to Matthew Aitken of Stock Aitken Waterman; he wrote for and produced many performers of the late 1980s, including Kylie Minogue and Jason Donovan. The building has two wings: Park Cottage (to the east) and West Cottage.

Nos.23-29 form a row of four stuccoed early-1850s houses built as Caen Terrace.

Lionel Salter (1914–2000), a musician who had a long career as a music administrator for the BBC, died at **No.25**. In the 1870s John Bradley Dyne Jr (see p 24) was living at No.27 (then No.3 Caen Terrace). Nos.31-33 are neo-Jacobean houses dating from the early 1870s and in the same style as Nos.14-22 on the north side. They were built over the site of Fitzroy Nursery, which had been run until 1858 by the Stein family, who had also managed the nursery on Highgate Green. **No.31** was initially called Highwood and has a prominent glazed attic, possibly once used as an artist's studio. Sir Frederick William Andrewes (1859–1932), pathologist and bacteriologist, lived here at the turn of the 20th century, when he was a noted lecturer at St Bartholomew's medical school. His son, Sir Christopher Andrewes (1896-1988), a virologist who became deputy director of the Medical Research Council, spent his childhood here. The young Christopher was often ill and forced to stay for many weeks in bed at home, where he watched and recorded the wildlife in the garden below. Until the end of his life he was able to identify by its botanical or common name any plant that was brought to him. **No.33** was first called Coombe House. The Congregational minister Alexander Mackennal (1835–1904) died here. He was a leader of the National Council of the Evangelical Free Churches, serving as its secretary from 1892 to

1898 and its president in 1899. William Young Hucks, for many years High Bailiff of Clerkenwell Court, died at No.33 in January 1933.

Nos.35-37 are the remnants of an early Victorian terrace of four houses called Park Terrace (Nos.1&2), extensively reconstructed in the 1880s, when Nos.3&4 were demolished and the semi-detached Stormont and Mansfield Villas built in their place. The latter are both long gone. In the 1890s Miss Henrietta Charles and her sister Janie lived with their mother at Stormont. In the previous decade the sisters had founded the Santa Claus Society, which distributed gifts to sick children in hospital, and in 1891 they set up a Santa Claus Home for Sick Children in a private house in South Grove. The home moved to Cholmeley Park, off Highgate Hill, in 1900 and was last operating in 1953, having by then become part of the NHS.

No.35 was home in the 1950s and 1960s to the Conservative politician Patrick Jenkin (b 1926), later an important member of the Thatcher government but at that time a Hornsey Borough Councillor and from 1964 MP for Wanstead and Woodford. **No.37** was home to John Lacey, prominent in the Highgate Society. In 1962 his 18-year-old son Nicholas was detained in a Cuban gaol accused of spying; he was released a few weeks before the Cuban missile crisis.

Beyond Bishopswood Road we reach the Highgate School sports ground, and facing us on the Camden side is a long brick wall. It is punctuated by the entrance to **Beechwood**, guarded by statues of dogs atop posts, and a tile-hung lodge built in the early 20th century. A farmhouse called Sherricks was here in 1650. The name Sherricks derived from Sirewic, which in Old English meant "bright settlement". In 1226 William De Blemont (who gave his name to Bloomsbury) leased a 12-acre plot of land next to the grove of Sirewic to one Safugle, and gave the remainder of his lands in the north of Tottenhall manor to the Holy Trinity Priory, Aldgate. Sherricks was licensed as a pub in 1730. Its land passed to the Fitzroys in the 18th century when they were lords of Tottenhall manor. Charles Fitzroy (1737–97), army officer, later 1st Baron Southampton and treasurer to the profligate Prince of Wales, inherited it from his mother in 1768. Shortly before 1774 he built a 7-bayed Palladian villa just south of the farmhouse. This villa has been described in historical accounts variously as Fitzroy House and Southampton Lodge, while contemporary newspaper reports usually called it Fitzroy Farm (which was the name of the estate). Early-19th-century deeds show that it was officially called The Grove House (the name taken from a house in The Grove which Fitzroy purchased, see p 24). The house was remodelled by Henry Holland in the 1790s **[13]**, when Humphrey Repton improved the park, whose grounds had initially been landscaped with "serpentine sweeps" by Capability Brown. The Fitzroys lived here until the death at the house in 1810 of George Ferdinand, 2nd Baron Southampton, after which they let it to a series of tenants. The last was Henry Robarts, a banker, whose guests included Coleridge, Byron and Keats. The contents of the house were sold at auction in October 1825 and the house was demolished the following year.

Through the gates glimpse the exterior of 2-storeyed stuccoed Beechwood, built over the site of the Fitzroys' house in 1838-1840. The exterior is little changed, but the interior was completely remodelled in the 20th century. The house was designed by George Basevi for his brother Nathaniel. The Basevis were a distinguished Anglo-Jewish family – an aunt was Disraeli's mother – but the brothers were both converted Christians and George was able to send his five sons to Highgate School. Nathaniel Basevi, a Lincoln's Inn barrister, married a niece of Sir Robert Peel, who often visited the house and is said to have suggested its name. Later residents included (from 1859) William Piper, the public works contractor and builder of Portsmouth Docks; and, from 1911 until his death, the coal merchant

13 Fitzroy Park, showing the Fitzroys' villa after it was remodelled by Henry Holland (Heal Collection)

Edward Perronet Sells III (1845-1915). In 1856 his grandfather, Edward Perronet Sells I had merged the family business with Charrington's, who dropped the Sells name in 1919 when his son, Edward Perronet Sells IV retired through ill health. Mrs Edward Perronet Sells III was chair of the Highgate 1919 Club, founded just after WWI as a social centre for the amusement and recreation of domestic servants. Oscar Lewis, son of John Lewis of the department store, and a big game hunter, arrived at Beechwood in 1929. From that year until 1945 he was Conservative MP for Colchester. In the late 1970s there were concerns locally about extensions and alterations made to the house in preparation for its occupation by King Khalid of Saudi Arabia (1912-82). His personal helicopter is not remembered fondly by Highgate locals. By 1986 Beechwood was owned by the Emir of Qatar, Khalifa bin Hamad al-Thani, who was given planning permission to convert the cottage in the grounds into staff accommodation.

A string of ponds formed after WWI lie at the foot of its large grounds, which enclose a large swimming pool dating from the time of Oscar Lewis as well as an immense beech tree. An 18th-century underground ice-house, a survival from the time of the Fitzroys, was recorded in the grounds in the late 1970s.

Continue, with the wall opposite. Some way further on, the wall incorporates a derelict outbuilding, crenellated and with fancy brick patterning. This was the coach-house of Caen Wood Towers, the large house with a big square tower away to the right; and just to the left is its bricked-up former entrance. There was once also a thatched entrance lodge here.

To build Caen Wood Towers and form its grounds, two 19th-century mansions were demolished: Dufferin Lodge and Fitzroy House. Dufferin Lodge, built in 1838-39 by the merchant Charles Crawley, was set in 4-acre grounds which were entered at this point. The house became the suburban residence of Lord Dufferin (1826-1902), who enjoyed, or suffered, the improbably long name of Frederick Temple Hamilton-Temple-Blackwood. He was later Governor General of Canada and Viceroy of India. He lived here with his devoted widowed mother Helen Selina, an author and songwriter, who was the granddaughter of Richard Brinsley Sheridan. She published songs and verses anonymously. George Hay, Earl of Gifford, had been her friend and suitor for some 15 years when in 1862 he was seriously injured by holding back a stone which was falling on some of his workmen. She decided the time had come to marry him; they were wed on 13 October 1862 at Dufferin Lodge but he died at the house on 22 December. She herself died here five years later from breast cancer. Another future Viceroy of India was born at Dufferin Lodge: Charles Hardinge (1858–1944), the second son of the 2nd Viscount Hardinge of Penshurst; his diplomatic career was advanced by Lord Dufferin. In 1860 the first garden show of the Highgate Horticultural Society, formed the year before, took place in the grounds. The shows became great annual events and no fewer than 12 shows were afterwards held in the grounds of Caen Wood Towers. The contents of Dufferin Lodge were auctioned off at the house in 1872, after which it was demolished.

Past the bus stop are the locked gates to the red-brick 'Jacobethan' building now called **Athlone House**, with its gatehouse alongside. This was initially the site of Fitzroy House, erected in 1838 by the solicitor George Abraham Crawley – brother of Charles – in whose memory the Crawley Chapel of Highgate School was built (p 21). After George died in 1863, his 8-acre estate was described at auction as Fitzroy Farm. The house was pulled down in 1869. The present mansion was built (1870-72) as Caen Wood Towers by Edward Salomons and John Philpot Jones for Edward Brooke, the Manchester-born entrepreneur who patented magenta and other dyes.

It has been described as a Victorian businessman's dream house. It was richly carved within [14] and had much stained glass, some by Morris & Co. The Brooke family lived here in grand style, with a large retinue of staff. It was subsequently owned

by a succession of prosperous businessmen such as Francis Reckitt (maker of the dye) and Sir Cory Francis Cory-Wright, a wealthy coal merchant who was High Sheriff of Middlesex and prominent in local affairs as Chairman of Hornsey Urban District Council. He died at the house in 1909. In WWI Belgian refugees were quartered at Caen Wood Towers, which was then turned into the American Hospital for British soldiers. It was later home to Sir Robert Waley-Cohen (1877-1952), its last private owner, who lived quite modestly here. The Shell Oil industrialist came from a wealthy family who had long been leaders of the Anglo-Jewish community. For nearly 40 years he was the chief figure of the United Synagogue and died in office as its president. His marriage ended tragically when his wife Alice died as a result of a motor accident in Palestine in 1935, in which Waley-Cohen himself was seriously injured. In 1951 the house was leased by the Ministry of Health, and was

14 Caen Wood Towers,
view of an interior

used by Middlesex Hospital as a nursing home. One resident was Wilfred, Lord Brown of Macrihanish (1908-65), a Privy Councillor who published many books on management and died at the home.

Athlone House was sold by the NHS in 2004, and is currently undergoing redevelopment. The large post-war NHS buildings adjoining it were removed in 2006, and 3 low blocks housing 22 flats and underground parking will be built in the grounds. One hectare of land has been donated by the developers to Hampstead Heath and the deeds of a small plot in the lower grounds were awarded to a squatter in May 2007 after he had lived there for 20 years. The original proposal was for the main house to be renovated to the designs of David Chipperfield as a 7-bed property, but during 2007 the house was sold separately and its future is uncertain.

Continue and then (dodging traffic!) cross over to the wall where it encloses a small brick house, **Caen Cottage**, part of the Athlone House estate. This is also to be renovated and extended. After this, the road continues towards Hampstead and in a few hundred metres passes the last house in Highgate, **Kenwood House**. Although we will shortly give a brief overview of its history, we shall not visit the house. Instead we take the sloping asphalt path on the left (*but see the note below*), down through a wooded area called The Orchard. From here there is a closer view, through the

trees, of Athlone House. At the bottom continue, with the fence of Athlone House's grounds to your left, and out onto Hampstead Heath, where the path becomes a narrow track. Sheep were a common sight here until the 1950s. Away to your right on the top of the slope is a copper-topped pergola near Kenwood.

Note that in winter months this path over the Heath can be quite muddy. To avoid this hazard, a rather long detour can be made: remain on Hampstead Lane, continuing beside the wall sheltering the former kitchen garden of Kenwood and taking the first broad turning left (Cut Through Lane), by the side of a telephone box near the house itself. Then proceed straight ahead, out onto the Heath on an asphalted footpath that eventually becomes a gravel lane. This detour has the advantage that it affords an exhilarating panorama of central London (whose landmarks are pointed out on a plaque in the pergola), and a fine prospect left towards St Michael's Church and Witanhurst. Another bonus is that lower down, where the footpath bends to the left by Millfield Gate, a few steps right will give you a view of the garden front of Kenwood, as well as the Sham Bridge behind the pond; and once we proceed left downhill there is good view of the rear of Athlone House. Those taking this detour rejoin the main route just past the Goodison fountain mentioned below.

For up to 300 years until the dissolution of the monasteries the area of Kenwood was owned by the Priory of Holy Trinity,

Aldgate. It was managed woodland. In 1525 a grant was made by the Prior to Nicholas Gray, yeoman of Highgate, "of the office of woodwardship, bailyship and keeping of their two woods Cane Wood and Gyll Holt". This is the first record of either name being used, but no description was given. Gray was the last woodward appointed by the Priory, which was dissolved in 1532. Within the next few years Cane Wood and Gyll Holt (about 190 acres of woodland) were leased to John Stannyng, one of the new class of gentry landowners looking for investment; he found it more profitable to sell the timber and use the land for grazing. Over the next 150 years many acres of ancient woodland disappeared. When Stannyng's lease expired in 1565, Cane Wood was sold and then resold in 1616 to John Bill, the King's printer, who probably built the first Kenwood House and cleared part of the wood. His son John Bill Jr, who inherited the estate, was a royalist who was imprisoned for his views. Gyll Holt was still there in 1685 when Lady Diana Bill surrendered her rights in Cane Wood to her son, Charles, who sold the house and land in 1690. Today there is no trace of Gyll Holt in the field names. In the early medieval period the name indicated a wooded valley, usually with a stream. It was probably a wood of willows and alders, trees which would have grown well in the damp ground of the valley ahead, in contrast to the oak ('keynes' in Norman French) of the higher, drier sandy soil which may have given Cane Wood its name.

One night in January 1661 after an engagement with the City militia, the insurrectionist "Fifth Monarchy men", led by Thomas Venner, took refuge in Cane Wood. Some of them were taken prisoner the next morning and the rest were dispersed. Venner himself was hanged, drawn and quartered, his fate witnessed by Pepys. His head was the last to be displayed on old London Bridge.

From 1712 Kenwood belonged to a succession of Scots, including the 2nd Duke of Argyll and his nephew, John, Lord Bute, the unpopular politician. Bute sold it to William Murray in 1754, the year Murray was appointed Attorney General. He subsequently became Lord (later 1st Earl) Mansfield and Lord Chief Justice, and lived partly in Bloomsbury Square and increasingly at Kenwood. His 1772 judgement ruling that a master could not dispatch a slave of his by force out of the country aided the abolitionist cause without espousing it or actually pronouncing slavery illegal. His carefully balanced judgements about slavery may have been due to the ambivalence he felt as he brought up at Kenwood both the illegitimate black daughter of one nephew, Dido Belle, and Lady Elizabeth Murray, the white daughter of his other nephew. He educated Dido

and used her as his amanuensis in later life. Mansfield employed Robert Adam to remodel the house in the fashionable neoclassical style. In the early 1770s the future architect of St Pancras New Church, William Inwood, was born at Kenwood, his father being Mansfield's bailiff. During the Gordon Riots of 1780 a mob suspecting Mansfield of being a Jacobite (like his father) and a Papist destroyed his London house and marched on Kenwood; they were diverted from their purpose by the landlord of the Spaniards inn, providing free ale by the roadside.

Mansfield's nephew Lord Stormont succeeded him as the 2nd Earl of Mansfield. In the 1790s he consulted Humphrey Repton about remodelling the grounds, persuading the authorities to move Hampstead Lane away from the house. The Mansfields eventually became absentee landlords, preferring to live at the family home at Scone Palace, Perthshire; Kenwood was let to tenants by the early 20th century. From 1910 to 1920 Kenwood was home to Grand Duke Michael (1861-1929), exiled from Russia because he married a mere countess. He and his wife were popular residents and gave lavishly to local charities (including giving the first motorised ambulance in London to Camden) until the Russian revolution spelt the end of much of his fortune. The Mansfields auctioned off the contents of the house in 1922 and the land was pegged

out in building plots. The actions of the Kenwood Preservation Council (see below) prevented this development. In 1924 the house and its surrounding grounds were purchased by Cecil Guinness, 1st Earl of Iveagh, who bequeathed them and his considerable art collection to the public upon his death in 1927.

Continue straight on. This part of the Heath, which until 1840 was the western part of the Fitzroys' parkland, is now known as Cohen's Fields, after Sir Robert Waley-Cohen, who was active in the campaign to save the Kenwood estate. You shortly pass two water-filled scrapes that were recently dug to encourage bogginess and attract birds and dragonflies to the area. The scrapes replace a pond lost to development at Athlone House. In winter, you can also make out the ruins of a Model Farm built in the grounds of Caen Wood Towers in the late 19th century. These are to be retained as a folly. Behind the hedge is a conservation area (not open to the public), part of the hectare of land donated by the Dwyer PLC, the present owners of Athlone House, who have also given £50,000 to the Corporation of London for its upkeep. The rest of the donated land, once again part of the Heath, can be reached by a (longish) detour left at the junction of footpaths beyond the large oak tree, over a small bridge, bearing left to reach, eventually, a small gate in the chestnut paling which gives access to the garden at the foot of the grounds of Athlone House.

Continue on the main path for another 100 metres to reach a circular basin with a fountain. This is known as the **Goodison fountain**. It was erected in 1929 to the memory of Henry Edmund Goodison, and presented by his wife and sons. This stockbroker was treasurer of the Kenwood Preservation Council, for whom he was an energetic fundraiser. Admire the strong carving, noting the wild animals – hedgehog, owl, stoat and squirrel – that nestle on swags between the heads of satyrs. The fountain is fed by a chalybeate spring, for which Hampstead became famous, and you can see the effect of the iron in the water by the staining on the basin.

The Kenwood Preservation Council was the brainchild of Sir Arthur Crosfield of Witanhurst (p 68), who launched it in 1919 with the help of Waley-Cohen, Goodison and Lawrence Chubb, the founder of the Ramblers Association, to whom a bench near Kenwood is dedicated. Crosfield (remembered at Kenwood by a plaque) masterminded a campaign involving royalty, nobility and multi-millionaires to save Lord Mansfield's lands from development. When he was unable to raise sufficient funds to buy the estate outright, Crosfield employed the tactic of buying it piecemeal so that housing development was less likely. The 88 acres of South Meadow (the land to the south of the Kenwood grounds) and Cohen's Fields were purchased in 1922

and the remaining 32 acres of woodland in 1924. The Kenwood Preservation Council, secure in the not then public knowledge that the Earl of Iveagh had negotiated the purchase of Kenwood, disbanded itself and handed its acquisitions over to the LCC for the enjoyment of the public.

A few steps farther on we join a broad gravel path forming a roadway. Turn left along it. This was the old track from Kentish Town to the Bishop of London's park (possibly also part of a drover's route from Finchley to the City). In its lower reaches ahead it becomes present-day **Millfield Lane**. It was known as Sherewick Lane (from Sirewic) until the 16th century. On the terrier to the 1804 Thompson map the land hereabouts is described as the "One Pond Field including the road [with] waste adjoining" which, as Richardson notes, indicates that this must have been a public road in medieval times, and as such may have been the original route up the hill. This section of the old road is now known locally as Nightingale Lane, alluding to John Keats' famous *Ode*. Here in April 1819, while out walking together, Coleridge and Joseph Green encountered Keats "the loose, sleek, not well-dressed youth", whom Green taught at Guy's. "There is death in that hand", Coleridge whispered to his companion, although Keats was then apparently in perfect health. Leigh Hunt called the track Poets' Lane, as Coleridge, Lamb and Hazlitt all frequented the area,

and the poet Coventry Patmore recalled in old age his "unspeakably happy walks in Millfield Lane".

Proceed under trees, with railings to the right. In a few minutes pass **Stock Pond**, the first of the series of Highgate Ponds, this one sometimes algae-covered and always very still. In 1693 William Paterson, who also helped found the Bank of England, founded the Society of Hampstead Aqueducts, more usually known as the Hampstead Waterworks Company. Its purpose was to supply water to London by using the various tributaries of the River Fleet to form ponds; the Highgate Ponds were in use as reservoirs by 1698. Fishing was strictly prohibited. In 1756 one James Andrews of Highgate was caught doing so and forced to make a public apology in lieu of punishment. The Society was incorporated into the New River Company in 1859. The water was never very drinkable and was last used, mainly for industry, in 1936.

Beyond the Stock Pond a path leads off to the right. We however continue ahead and pass round a barrier. On our left are the garden fences and walls of properties that lie off Fitzroy Park. The first two sets of gates are the rear entrances to **Fitzroy Farm**, whose gables can be made out. Here stood an ancient farmhouse taken over by the Fitzroys, who erected numerous outbuildings. The Fitzroys ran their farmland as a dairy farm **[15]**, at that time a fashionable pastime for noble ladies. There was a great rivalry between Lady Southampton and Lady Mansfield (Louisa, wife of the 2nd Earl) over the quality of their respective dairy herds. The farm and yards were sold to Lord Mansfield in 1840, and tenant farmers – the Ward family –

were here until WWI. Their farm was very picturesque, as old photos attest. Its flagged yard contained a quaint wooden granary on stone supports. The farm closed in 1923, Lord Mansfield having sold the freehold. Five years later the farmhouse was extended in Tudor style for residential use. It was

15 'A general view of Highgate taken from near the south-east corner of Caen Wood', drawn in 1786 (Wallis Bequest). The farm buildings in the middle ground are those of Fitzroy Farm.

mostly destroyed in a fire in the 1970s but reconstructed as before, using many of the 16th-century timbers. In the 1980s the owner, Mr Lathyrus, a Greek shipping magnate, tried unsuccessfully to have street lights put along the lane outside. Camden Council decided that this would change its character, a ruling upheld on appeal in February 1986. Planning permission has recently been granted for the demolition of the property and its replacement by a neo-Palladian house designed in the Corinthian order by the architect Quinlan Terry.

On the right is the main entrance to the **Kenwood Ladies' Bathing Pond** (unseen from the path). This part of the Kenwood estate came into public ownership in 1925 and a ladies' pond was opened by King George V and Queen Mary the following year. In the early years there was a Kenwood Regulars' Swimming Club – the appositely-named Laura Toplis being the secretary – in which the women members wore brightly coloured wool costumes they had knitted themselves. In 1934, in response to a request from users, nude sunbathing was prohibited, but ladies have been allowed to go topless since the long hot summer of 1976. The pond has a proper poolside deck, with diving areas and fixed ladders, and cubicles for changing.

On the left is the gate to **The Water House**, which overlooks an ancient pond that lies behind the fence. This modern house, constructed in the late 1990s, is on

the site of a farm building shown on the 1804 map which was formerly known as Fitzroy Farm Cottage. In the 19th century this was a *cottage orné* with an arched loggia. William Turner Warwick, senior surgeon at Middlesex Hospital and a national authority on the treatment of varicose veins, lived at Fitzroy Farm Cottage until his death in 1949. Before the late 1830s there met at a three-way junction at this point (a) the entrance to the Fitzroys' park, whose carriageway skirted the pond before proceeding up the hill to the east, (b) the entrance to Fitzroy Farm and (c) the route we have just traversed, the way up to Kenwood.

The lane now rises and before it joins the road, a path on the right leads onto the Heath between **Bird Sanctuary Pond** and the model boating pond (p 75). For centuries this has been a favourite route for walkers between Highgate and Hampstead. From 1904 the Mansfield (Highgate) Rifle Club – for female shooting fans – was based at a miniature rifle range just off to our right, by the side of the former pond. The club did not survive WWI.

We now turn sharp left into **FITZROY PARK**, a private, unadopted road. This lower stretch was first laid out in the late 1830s to link up to the old carriageway of the Fitzroys' house. Until the mid-20th century Fitzroy Park was a secluded country lane, which became a favoured place for architects to build houses for

themselves. Even though a fair number have been built along it, it is still an umbrageous promenade.

The first house on the left on a triangular site is **Apex Lodge**. It began life in the 1830s as a lodge to the Fitzroys' park; note the remnants of a 19th-century bargeboard on the original building on the left. The house was extensively renovated in 2006. Beyond lies **Fitzroy Lodge**, an interwar building somewhat in the style of Lutyens, with an elaborate hooded porch. Reg Connelly, part of a musical partnership that wrote songs such as *Show Me the Way to Go Home* and *Goodnight Sweetheart*, was living here in 1937. It was later home until her death of the cardiologist Dame Frances Gardner (1913-89). She was consultant physician at the Royal Free Hospital for 30 years and also dean of the medical school from 1962 to 1975. Retirement allowed more time for her other passion of gardening and the tending of her allotment which, though close to home, she reached on an electric milk float.

Then comes flat-roofed **No.55** (otherwise Tirnanog), a relatively small 1950s house with a huge back garden. This encloses the large pond overlooked by The Water House, remaining from the time of the Fitzroys; it then lay at the foot of a long narrow stretch of woodland called The Dingle that ran eastward as far as Highgate village. On the right are three detached interwar properties. **Kenview** is in International Style, as is **Sunbury** further along; these two sandwich Voysey-inspired **Ashridge**. Kenview was home to Sidney Leader Cramer, managing director of the tailoring firm Austin Reed and for many years Chairman of the Fitzroy Park Residents' Association. Ernest Marcus Gollance MBE, eldest son of the rabbi Sir Hermann Gollancz and first cousin of the publisher and writer Victor Gollancz, died at his home Ashridge in August 1960. Opposite Sunbury, small and boxy, white-boarded **No.53** was built in 1952 by Stephen Gardiner.

On the right is **FITZROY CLOSE**, a collection of five modern detached houses, begun in the early 1970s to the designs of Ted Levy, Benjamin and Partners. **No.5** (on the left, not visible from Fitzroy Park) followed in the mid-1980s. **No.1** (also known as No.12 Fitzroy Park) was to have been replaced in 1997 with a neoclassical design by the Camden-based architects Jestico and Whiles; it was eventually demolished in 2003 and the present modernist structure erected by Square One architects. Its two pitched roofs are separated by a 2-storey obscure-glazed entrance porch and its facing of horizontally laid black slates is very striking.

Continue towards the bend in **FITZROY PARK**, passing on the left No.51 and, nestling at the foot of the slope, **No.49**, a substantial mock-Tudor house built in 1930, with a tall chimney and

several roof windows that gave the house its name, Dormers. After **Farm End Cottage** on the corner, built at about the same time, take a short detour left, to take in the car park and pavilion of the **North London Bowling Club**. The club was founded in 1891, when it rented from farmer Tom Ward a piece of meadowland, which it levelled and made into a bowling green. A pavilion was formed from a cowshed; its current successor was built soon after WWI. Mrs Ward provided catering for the club, where her husband was a member. The Bowling Club was incorporated in 1924 in order to acquire the freehold of the land.

The roadway here leads to Fitzroy Farm (p 60) and two other houses: the **Little House** (a small pitched-roof building by the road, which was built in the 1950s as the guest house for Fitzroy Farm) and, behind the gateway, the **Wallace House**. This took its name from its then owners, who in 1998 remodelled an earlier structure called simply The Bungalow. They had to retain the façade, but within they opted for a minimalist, open-plan design with liberal use of glass surfaces.

Return to the bend. On our left is the large **Lodge**, in an early-20th-century cottage style. The core of the house was once a lodge to Caen Wood Towers, because the road to our left was first formed as the rear carriageway of 19th-century Fitzroy House, which Caen Wood Towers replaced. One of its

roofs is surmounted by a horse-shaped weathervane. Walk past the Lodge to view the trio of larger detached houses built down this side road in the 1930s. These are **Westwind**, **Dancers End** (probably named after the hamlet above Tring in Hertfordshire) and **Kenbrook**, with its rough-timbered gable and outsize garage block alongside. Kenbrook was home to Sir Bertrand Watson (1878-1948), Chief Metropolitan Magistrate from 1941; in 1945 he committed 'Lord Haw Haw' (William Joyce) to trial for high treason at the Central Criminal Court.

Go back to the main section of Fitzroy Park and turn uphill to the left. This is the route of the Fitzroys' carriageway, which was tree-lined. The land on our left was the easternmost of that bought by the Earl of Mansfield in the 1840 sale, although by the late 19th century it was leased to the owners of Caen Wood Towers. The land was secured by the Kenwood Preservation Council in 1922 and sub-sold to St Pancras Borough with a restriction on building. St Pancras soon afterwards laid out these allotments. The 86 plots are eagerly sought after, and there is a 10-year waiting list.

Behind the wall to our right once lay Southampton Lodge **[16]** and its extensive grounds. It was built in 1845 and was the home from 1847 until his death of the Volunteer Rifles' commander Colonel Josiah Wilkinson (1812-1903). He was a long-time member of the Metropolitan

Board of Works, representing St Pancras. His son Neville, born here in 1869, became an army officer and Ulster King of Arms; he announced the accession of King George V.

The gardens were very beautiful in Wilkinson's time; he had employed Robert Marnock, one of the leading garden designers of the day (although they later fell out). The Southampton Lodge estate was put up for auction in 1906, the prospectus extolling its gardens and grounds and noting its model cow farm and piggeries. There were no takers and it was again auctioned in 1908. The following year the Cutbush firm (p 70) built a huge greenhouse in the grounds; this was run as the Highgate Nursery, which could also be entered from Merton Lane (p 74). The estate was sold again in 1918 to Michael Embiricos, a wealthy Greek shipowner, and once more in early 1923 to Sir Robert Waley-Cohen of Caen Wood Towers. The southern parts of the grounds adjoining Merton Lane were then sold off; the house itself divided into three residences and into five by the 1930s. Flat No.1 was home to Sir Robert Waley-Cohen in his last years; he died here in November 1952. The house was demolished in 1960.

Follow the long stretch of cobbles, which enclose two trees. These bear plaques erected by the Fitzroy Park Residents' Association to commemorate two notable members – Dame Frances Gardner and Sidney Leader Cramer,

whose homes we have already passed. The cobbles lead into the courtyard of Grade-II-Listed **No.10**, a low neo-Georgian brick house with very tall chimneys. It has something about it of Lutyens, including

16 Southampton Lodge
(pictured in the sale particulars, 16 July 1906)

the specially made Roman-style bricks. Note the keystone above the door, carved with a coat of arms featuring hedgehogs and a castle. A hedgehog is known in heraldry as a herisson and was often chosen by those surnamed Harrison or Harris.

No.10 was built in 1932-34 by the

workaholic civic architect (Emmanuel) Vincent Harris (1876–1971) as his own house. It lies on the site of the former Cutbush greenhouse, Harris having purchased 1¾ acres of the Southampton Lodge estate. The house was largely designed by Donald McMorran, one of several talented architects who assisted Harris in his busiest years. In 1938 Vincent's mother Mary Harris died here after breaking her leg in a fall, at the advanced age of 104. In 1952 her son decided, because of all the commissions he had received, to bequeath the house, along with his Daimler, to St Pancras Council upon his death. In 1953, at the auction following Waley-Cohen's demise, Harris bought Southampton Lodge in order to extend his garden, on condition that St Pancras demolish the Lodge, which they duly did seven years later.

However, other conditions attached to the bequest proved more problematic. Harris insisted that No.10 be used as a mayoral residence, or else for educational or arts purposes; but its location was not practical for the latter, and no mayor chose to live here. Camden Council (the successor body to St Pancras) took nearly ten years after Harris's death to decide to use it as a training centre. In 1992 the Council tried unsuccessfully to remove the covenants so that it could sell the house, after which it was used until 2000 by a horticultural training scheme for young people. The Council subsequently went ahead and sold the house (often referred to in Council reports, rather oddly, as Fitzroy House) for single-family occupation, with the proviso that the original garden be preserved. The proceeds were put into a charity fund for Camden, appropriately

named the Emmanuel Vincent Harris Fund.

Beyond are the half-dozen private houses of the cul-de-sac **THE HEXAGON**, almost lost in trees and shrubbery. The flat-roofed 2-storey houses in brick with timber cladding were built at the start of the 1960s by Leonard Michaels. The first occupant of **No.1** was the scientist and writer Sir Jacob Bronowski (1908-74). The Hexagon lies on the site of a villa called Hillside, erected soon after 1840. For a decade from 1844 this was home to the painter Margaret Gillies (1803–87) and her partner, the physician (Thomas) Southwood Smith (1788–1861) **[17]**, who had separated from his second wife. Gillies was a portraitist and her sitters included Leigh Hunt, Charles Dickens, William Wordsworth and Jeremy Bentham, whose utilitarian ideas strongly influenced Southwood Smith in his pioneering public health work. Also living here was Margaret's elder sister Mary Gillies (1800–70). She had a relationship with the children's writer Richard Henry Horne, whose *A New Spirit of the Age*, which included engravings from four portraits by Margaret, appeared in 1844 when he, too, was living at Hillside. Gertrude Hill, Southwood Smith's granddaughter whom he adopted, lived with Margaret Gillies and continued to do so even after her marriage in 1865 to Charles Lee Lewes, the son of George Eliot's lover. Gertrude's sister Octavia Hill was early involved in

her grandfather's philanthropic work and became a notable figure in the housing movement. As children, Gertrude and Octavia were excited about the visit to Hillside of Hans Christian Andersen, but found him unexpectedly stiff and silent. In the 1880s Gertrude and her husband Charles Lee Lewes returned to live at the house. Lewes was a member of the LCC and a leader in the fight to save Parliament Hill Fields. Another resident who helped to save part of Hampstead Heath for the public was Henry Edmund Goodison, here from 1910, whose memorial fountain we saw earlier. Hillside was demolished during the 1950s.

Continue up sylvan **FITZROY PARK**. On the right, the site of The Limes is now covered by trees and undergrowth. The house dated from 1846 and was called Fitzroy Farm Cottage by its first occupant, Lewis Hertslett. He was secretary to the Metropolitan Board of Works and his father of the same name was Foreign Office librarian and editor of state papers. The local historian Lloyd wrote in the 1880s that this "cottage in a dell" was popularly known as Honeymoon Villa. It was pulled down in 1954.

Beyond the allotments on the left are **No.**7 and the smaller **No.**7A, called The Vinery. Both date from 1957 and were designed by June Park – No.7 for herself and her architect husband Cyril Mardall (who added an extension with big brick piers to the west in the 1960s); and No.7A for her mother. Extensive basement work was being undertaken at No.7 in 2007. Beyond are a single-storey lodge and the stuccoed brick gateposts of the now disused southern entrance to The Elms (see below), all Listed Grade II.

Some way further on, on the right, is the securely gated **HIGHFIELDS GROVE**, a modern enclave of large detached houses. These were built in the mid-1980s, in the face of much local opposition, in the lower grounds of Witanhurst (p 68). Brick-built in six different styles, they were designed by Rottenberg Associates.

On the left side of **FITZROY PARK** note two large buildings currently being extensively renovated, with a third also being restored. That nearest us is **The Elms**, to which the second building is linked. As Elm Lodge, this Grade-II-Listed villa was built for himself in 1838-40 by the architect George Basevi (1794-1845), a pupil of John Soane. Many of his projects came to him through his extensive family connections. They included work at country houses and most notably the development of Belgrave Square. The Fitzwilliam Museum, Cambridge is his best-known and most successful work, in many ways realising Soane's own ideal of a public architecture based on the fullest interpretation of the ruins of imperial Rome. Basevi's career was cut short when he fell to his death through an opening in the floor of the old bell chamber in the west tower of Ely Cathedral while inspecting repairs.

William Gladstone, an East India merchant and first cousin of the prime minister of the same name, lived here from 1847. Subsequent residents included Samuel Pope QC, and Otto Gossell, the iron and steel merchant who died here in 1888 and had initially called the house Sunny Side. In the first years of the 20th century the house was renamed The Elms. In the 1930s and 1940s Dr Peter Gorer (1907-61), an experimental pathologist at Guy's Hospital, lived in the house and his wife regularly opened its gardens to the public. In 1944 the couple were both injured in a car accident, as was their passenger Ernest Hemingway, who sustained head injuries. From 1950 The Elms was home to the Botswana-born solicitor Ambrose Appelbe (1903-99). His clients included the mass murderer John Christie, who left him his half-moon reading glasses (which Appelbe would often wear) and Mandy Rice-Davies, whom he guided through the Profumo Affair. He was also an inveterate founder of causes, some worthy, some eccentric. He helped found the National Marriage Guidance Council (now known as Relate), Help the Aged, War on Want, the Youth Hostels Association and the Anti-Noise Society. In 1935, with George Bernard Shaw and H G Wells, he set up the (ultimately unsuccessful) Smell Society, which sought to eliminate foul odours. Appelbe failed to maintain his house well, splitting much of it up into 9 flats with flimsy partitions. In December 1987 The Elms was bought by a multi-millionaire member of the Saudi royal family, who intended to turn it into his main European residence. The suitably palatial leisure complex planned for the site met stiff local opposition and plans were revised and approved which included a large sports pavilion and two mansions in the grounds. Neither was built and the house lay dilapidated for much of the 1990s, while the owner lived elsewhere. In 2002 it was bought by a Russian for £20m with the aim of restoring and extending it; work is currently underway, to designs by Alan Power.

Next, alongside the roadway, is 19th-century stuccoed **Elm Cottage**. This was originally the coach house of The Elms, at its northern entrance. It was home to the actor-producer Ronald Shiner (1903-66) from 1951 until a year before his death. Shiner made over 200 films and had his own TV series. An article he wrote for the *St Pancras Journal* in 1962 revealed his love of Highgate.

Beyond Elm Cottage are outbuildings of Beechwood (p 54), one of which houses a squash court. Facing these, on the right, is **No.8A**, designed by Hal Higgins of Higgins, Ney and Partners in 1965-67. It is Listed Grade II. With its jagged profile, it exploits the slope of the hill. Built for P Epstein, an American engineer who had a large household, it has a dramatic layout: a glass-encased living space is surrounded by five separate pavilions. It was being renovated in 2007 by the architectural firm Studio Mark Ruthven. **No.8** by the bend

also has angular roofing. It was built in 1953, as his own house, by the architect Cecil George Stillman (1894-1968). County architect of Middlesex at the time, he was well known for designing schools, and credited with initiating a prefabricated approach during the 1930s which enabled new systems to be devised in the post-war period. On the corner across from No.8 is the rear entrance to Beechwood; alongside is **Beechwood Cottage**, an interwar neo-Georgian building.

The road bends to the right and rises ever more steeply. The houses beyond on the left include **The Summit**, built in 1915 in an Arts and Crafts manner, and rather blank 1950s **No.3** (Tregoze), with a back entrance to Park Villa (p 53). **Birch House**, large-eaved with tall chimneys, was put up in 1998 by the owners of adjoining **No.1**. The latter was built in 1917 as Melrose; it was the home of Edith Summerskill (p 76) and her husband Jeffrey Samuel in the late 1930s, when they ran a medical partnership. After WWII the house was taken over by the Soviet Trade Delegation and split into flats; an extension was built in the early 1980s on the site of Birch House. In 1997 No.1 was restored as a single-family home.

Opposite is partially timber-clad **No.6**, end-on to the road and with a butterfly roof. It was designed by the Danish architect Erhard Lorenz in 1956-8 for his compatriot Ove Arup (1895-1988), the civil

engineer, who was involved in the design and construction of many world-famous projects including Highpoint flats and the Sydney Opera House. Arup was knighted in 1971 and died here seventeen years later. Eva Jiricina refurbished the interior in 1993-94 and added a minimalist glass wing with a gym overlooking the swimming pool.

At the top the roadway levels out and we pass an avenue of limes. On the right is a row of garages which conceal the entrance to **No.2**, a wide-fronted 1950s house designed by local architect June Park. The land here was once part of the 'Great Garden' of the first Grove House and was leased for building by the Fitzroy family from 1831. Pass round the barrier, by which there is a decayed wooden post which may date back to the time of the Fitzroys. We join The Grove (p 24). Turn left, then right, into Hampstead Lane to return to the Gatehouse, passing the site of Grove House at No.12 The Grove.

Alternatively, turn right to reach the corner with Highgate West Hill to continue exploring the former Fitzroy estate in Route 4.

Highgate West Hill and Millfield Lane

Downhill walk from the corner of The Grove and Highgate West Hill to Swain's Lane

For modern map see back cover

This walk covers the southern part of the Fitzroys' estate, which once stretched south as far as the River Fleet, at the foot of Highgate West Hill. The Fitzroys were Lords of the Manor of Tottenhall, and their estate in Highgate was demesne land, although the first 100 metres or so of this walk lies within what was once the adjoining manor of Cantelowes.

The walk begins at the edge of Highgate village at the junction of The Grove and **HIGHGATE WEST HILL**. The latter was usually called Highgate Hill until well into the 19th century (which must have caused considerable confusion), and it was not formally named West Hill until 31 January 1893. It was renumbered and renamed Highgate West Hill in 1939 when it absorbed part of South Grove, but we begin our walk where pre-WWII West Hill began.

The road is not as old as Millfield Lane (p 75) but it is shown on Norden's map of 1593. The crest of the hill here, however, is a place of settlement of considerable antiquity. By 1481 there were at least two houses at Dancok or Dancope Hill, as this area was then known. It was a favourite place for gravel diggers; in 1485 a tyler of Holloway was fined 4 shillings for taking gravel away without a licence. The hollow further down the hill, below Holly Lodge Gardens (p 105), may well have been caused by medieval gravel extraction.

At No.41, behind a 2-storey gatehouse by Seely & Paget, lies **Witanhurst**. This palatial neo-Georgian mansion, Listed Grade II★, was built for the soap magnate Sir Arthur Crosfield MP. It is said to be the largest private house in London after Buckingham Palace.

It lies on the site of Parkfield. Parkfield can be traced back to 1665 when Peter Sambrooke, a London apothecary, sold the property to Simon Baxter, a London draper. From 1774 it was owned by the Crutchfield family until it was sold in 1843 to the merchant Allen Williams Block. His major extensions to the house were continued by his brother-in-law, Walter Scrimgeour, barrister and stockbroker, to whom he sold it in 1889. The architect John Malcolm included in it a celebrated billiard room and gymnasium. Parkfield was sold again in 1912 to Sir Arthur Crosfield.

He retained a portion of Parkfield, which became the south-west wing of Witanhurst (on the left). It dates from about 1700 and is of red and brown brick. The rest of the present grandiose L-shaped building is in a similar style, 2- and 3-storeyed, with attics. It was constructed between 1913 and 1920 by George Hubbard for Crosfield, who chose its name by combining two Anglo-Saxon words, for *parliament* and *wooded hill*. The main front of Witanhurst, with an Ionic colonnade, faces west. Nothing of the 18th century survives internally in the old part, where much of the ground floor served as a billiard room after decoration had been carried out for Crosfield by Percy McQuoid. The mansion contains more than 50 rooms, including a neo-baroque staircase hall and a large north-western music room, with richly carved details.

Crosfield's highly successful family business produced chemicals and soap, including the brand called Perfection and from 1909 Persil (in the UK). The firm was based in Warrington, which he represented as Liberal MP from 1906 to 1910. It was sold in 1911 and is now part of Unilever, but Crosfield himself remained extremely rich until the 1930s. He was a Graecophile, campaigning for many Greek causes. The Greek Prime Minister Eleutherios Venizelos was married at Witanhurst in 1921, and Crosfield's young wife Domini came from the prominent Greek family of Elliardi. He is said to have built the house as a platform for her social ambitions. Here the Crosfields organised once famous tennis parties, held immediately before or after the Wimbledon tournament, in aid of charity. The guests came from society and royalty; Queen Elizabeth herself attended when she was a princess. Sir Arthur, whose last years were beset by financial disaster and depression, died in 1938 after falling (or jumping) from the midnight express train to Cannes. His widow remained at Witanhurst until her own death in 1963, continuing to hold annual tennis tournaments, as well as concerts in the music room.

The mansion overlooks 13 acres of well timbered grounds, which were laid out from 1914 onwards by the landscape architect Sir Harold Peto, with ornate gardens and tennis courts.

The family put the house on the market in 1965; after it was sold there was a vigorous and protracted local campaign to protect Witanhurst and its grounds from redevelopment. No fewer than three separate planning enquiries took place. The eventual outcome was that the house and its immediate surroundings were retained, but permission was given in 1982 for the erection of houses in the lower grounds – the development known as Highfields Grove (p 66). Witanhurst had been acquired by the Noble Company, a Kuwaiti-funded group, in the late 1970s, but has fallen into disrepair in recent years. In 2002-03 the BBC hired the house, at great expense, for its make-your-own popstar show, *Fame Academy*, and also filmed a number of period dramas here. In 2005 Witanhurst was put on the market with a cool £32 million price tag, on the understanding that several more millions would be needed to repair the damage caused by its standing empty for so long.

The area in front of the gates and on the corner of The Grove is the site of an Elizabethan building called the Blue House. This was the mansion of an estate of 38 acres adjoining Sherricks (p 54) to the west. At the start of the 17th century it was owned by the Warner family, who in 1620 conveyed it to Sir Robert Payne. He later sold it to Henry Pierrepont, Marquess of Dorchester (d.1680) and Lord of Cantelowes manor during the Commonwealth. The Blue House then became known as Dorchester House. This was a 3-storeyed mansion of brick with stone dressings designed by John Thorpe. The gardens were on two levels, with a brick wall for the upper terrace, part of which is still visible from houses in The Grove. By the early 1680s Dorchester House was owned by the City draper William Blake, who wanted to use it as part of his Ladies' Hospital, a charity school for City orphans (see p 25). The scheme ended in failure and bankruptcy for Blake, whose creditor Sir Francis Pemberton took over Dorchester House and demolished it by 1699. Built on its site by 1728 were two houses, one of which was later called Grove Bank. This was used for a variety of educational purposes for much of the 19th century, lastly as a girl's boarding school run by the Lacey sisters, who also used Nos.1&2 The Grove for school premises. Grove Bank was empty by 1929 and was demolished two years later to improve access to Witanhurst.

Continue past the gates of Witanhurst. Opposite, on the other side of the pedestrian crossing, is diminutive, cobbled **WITANHURST LANE**. A remnant of Bromwich Walk (p 106), it ends in the spiked gates of another significant building, which cannot be viewed from the road. This is **Bromwich House**, the only house in the lane, numbered No.1. It was completed in 1995, after nearly a decade's fight by its architect Elana Keats to gain planning permission. It is tucked into the south-facing slope of the hill and the entrance is at the top. It has two roof gardens and is set within 3 acres of grounds containing waterfalls and cascades. The house was built with Star-Trek style doors which open as one approaches the swimming pool complex.

Now proceed west along **HIGHGATE WEST HILL**, looking at the buildings opposite. Behind tall shrubbery is Grade II-Listed **Nos.78&79**, with gable windows and fishscale roof slates. The external chimney stack suggests the great age of the building. Occupying a site mentioned in 1493 where the inn the White Hart stood by 1664, the building is a late-18th-century conversion from three cottages. The White Hart itself was the easternmost of the cottages, where 17th-century timbering has been found. There are still large cellars underneath. The White Hart was leased to William Bowstread in 1780; Bowstread had a nursery here in 1804, the inn having closed. The nursery was subsequently taken over from 1822 by the aptly-named William Cutbush, whose horticultural skills were known all over London. In 1834 Cutbush built a new residence and shop at **No.80**, which is now also Listed Grade II. It has tall gables and prominent barge boards and is currently painted yellow. The tall trees beyond cover the site of a glass conservatory that fronted the road when the Cutbush firm was here **[18]**. The firm was known for its forced bulbs, especially hyacinths.

William Cutbush died in 1854 and his son James, a founding member of the Highgate Horticultural Society, went bankrupt in 1883 and died two years later. The firm was, however, continued by his grandsons William and Herbert, and again thrived. The Cutbush Highgate nursery gardens were based in the old kitchen gardens of Kenwood and for a time at Southampton Lodge (p 64); they had other branches in Barnet and Finchley. The shop on this site was closed in 1915 and the house became private. In the mid-1930s the actor Bobbie Howes (d.1972) was living at No.80, with a collection of noisy dogs, about whom his neighbours complained. The house was also rented at times by the Highgate Bridge Club.

18 Cutbush nursery buildings, West Hill (advertisement, 1887)

The hill soon begins its descent. The next run of buildings opposite is what appears to be an 18th-century terrace, Grade-II-Listed **Nos.81-83** shown on Thompson's 1804 map as Nos.1,2 & 3 Highgate Hill. Note the impressive iron gate to No.82, spear-headed and featuring fleur-de-lys; the porch has fluted columns and above the doorway is a Georgian fanlight. This house, also known as Hollyside, is on the site of property sold by William Cholmeley to Sir James Harrington of Swakeleys, Ickenham, in 1656. Harrington was one of the judges at the trial of Charles I and a conspicuous member of the Rump regime: he had to leave the country at the Restoration. The house was acquired in 1664 by

Francis Blake, gentleman, father of the above-mentioned William Blake. He conveyed it to Robert Osbaldeston who in 1712 also acquired the site of Holly Terrace (p 72) and 13 acres below it. This whole estate was owned by the Cooke family by 1741. Part of the old building survived in Hollyside. The house contains chimney-stacks of that date, although the internal features are mostly 18th-century. No.81 and No.83 both date from about 1794, but rebuilding in 1823 joined the latter to No.82. Lewis Vulliamy, the architect of St Michael's church, lived at No.81, also known as Reedsdale, from 1853 to 1857. At No.82 in the 1840s lived Francis Rivington (1805-85), of the famous publishing firm, at a time when its fortunes had been damaged by its association with the Tractarian movement in the Church of England. From 1910 until 1938 No.82 was home to Admiral Henry Purey-Cust, the hydrographer. John Betjeman had a boyhood crush on his daughter Peggy, immortalised in verse.

Beyond is the imposing 3-storeyed **No.84**. This Grade-II-Listed building, also known as Holmwood, started life as two houses built by 1710, which were amalgamated in 1824. The devout Quaker Sir Edward Fry (1827-1918), who became Lord Chief Justice, lived here in the early

19 The Fox & Crown, photographed by H R Gibbs shortly before its demolition (*Black and White*, 2 Nov 1895)

1860s. His daughter, the relief worker and social reformer Joan Mary Fry (1862-1955) was born here. From 1879 until his death in 1918 No.84 was the home of Robert Leabon Curtis JP, who was mayor of his native West Ham, the architect of St Joseph's schools and a promoter of Westminster Cathedral. From shortly before WWII until 2004 the house was used as a Youth Hostel.

Past the wall of Witanhurst on our side is **No.40**, now known as The Summit and containing a private health centre. It is the site of the Fox & Crown **[19]**, as a terracotta plaque on the present Arts and Crafts building attests. The pub closed in October 1895 to make way by 1898 for outbuildings and stables for the adjoining Parkfield. The inn had existed since the

17th century, after a piece of common land was enclosed here in 1663. Sometimes also known as the Fox under the Hill, it was first called the Fox & Crown in 1704. Just two weeks after her accession, Queen Victoria was returning from a drive with her mother when at the top of West Hill the wheel of the royal carriage broke off and the horses were about to bolt. The landlord Mr Turner managed to stop the carriage careering out of control down the hill. While the vehicle was being repaired, the young queen was recovering from the experience on a chair in the forecourt. She asked the landlord what favour he wanted in return, and he asked for the right to erect the royal coat of arms. This was granted; the arms are now in the HLSI. Turner's friends later suggested he should have asked for something more substantial, and he is said to have worried himself to an early grave.

No.39 is a pleasant Georgian house alongside the road. This was Sutton Cottage, which replaced two earlier tenements built on the common land. It probably dates from 1736 when Edward Yardley, a preacher at Highgate Chapel, lived here. In the 1760s it was owned by Henry Woodfall, the proprietor of the *Public Advertiser*. The painter James John Hill (1811-82) was here for 40 years from 1842, the year he was elected a member of the Society of British Artists. He was a frequent and popular contributor to its exhibitions.

He painted several pictures of horses and dogs for Baroness Burdett-Coutts, one of his most regular patrons. **No.38** was built in 1850, and at first named Cintra Cottage.

On the south side, opposite, are the rear entrances of houses in Holly Terrace (see below). **No.87**, for example, is also No.6 Holly Terrace, as painted on the entrance. Behind the gate on our side and set high above the road is tile-hung **No.37**, or West Lodge. This 1920s house replaced late-18th-century West Hill Lodge, occupied during the 1860s by the Howitts, William (1792-1879) and Mary (1792-1888). They wrote many books here, including *The Northern Heights of London*. The Howitts' blend of history, topography, spirituality and democratic politics was immensely popular in their day. Mary translated several of Hans Christian Andersen's works and wrote many children's books and poetry of her own; she penned *The Spider and the Fly*. Florence Nightingale stayed at their home in 1859 to recuperate after the Crimean War. The Howitts were in a good position to see the cruelty suffered by horses struggling up the hill, which they complained about in print. Horse transport had not yet been supplanted by motorised transport when in 1906 newspapers reported a novel and successful experiment: a 30hp omnibus achieved the ascent of Highgate West Hill from a standing start.

Beyond, notice in the wall some ornate rustication; this was the site of a drinking fountain. Here cross over to the bench opposite, where you may care to pause. On the bend ahead are two detached interwar properties: flat-roofed **No.36** and Wren-like **No.35A**, which was initially called Dunottar. With these houses we rejoin the former estate of the Fitzroys. The two houses were built in 1936 in the grounds of Highgate Lodge, a large villa demolished the previous year; it had been erected in 1829 by John Gordon. Its residents included Edward Atkinson, a gentleman who accompanied the then famous balloonist Henry Coxwell on several ascents, of which he published an account. Sir Horatio Regnart JP, vice-chairman of Maples and a St Pancras Alderman, lived here from 1889 until 1904, when it became the home of the millionaire shipowner Sir John Glover JP, chairman of Lloyds Register of Shipping. He celebrated his diamond wedding here in April 1914, but Lady Glover died at the house ten months later and Glover himself in 1920.

Now continue, turning the bend and shortly reach steps on your left. Go through the gate above them into the private pathway that is **HOLLY TERRACE**. Continue as far as No.8 ahead. The flagstones can be slippery after rain. There are eleven stuccoed houses, all Listed Grade II, several sporting splendidly ornate iron balconies and commanding fine views towards London. Nos.1-7 stand on the grounds of a large late-17th-century house, which from about 1797 to 1805 was occupied by Rev. Alexander Crombie, minister of Highgate Presbyterian church, who ran the Holly House Academy here. The house was demolished by 1813 and No.2 erected on its site; the rest of the south-facing terrace had already been formed in 1807 by George Smart for the owner of the land, John Cooke.

The writer George Burgin (1856-1944) lived at **No.2** from 1907-22 and subsequently at No.8 from 1923 until WWII. His output, mainly sentimental novels, was prodigious. He always wore a fez and wrote that "it is much more comfortable to be mad and know it than to be sane and have one's doubts". At **No.3** from 1907 lived Ernest Harrington, whose wife was a leading local suffragette. An early occupant of **No.4** was the Unitarian minister and writer Jeremiah Joyce (1763–1816), who had been imprisoned in the Tower for high treason for preaching against the European reaction to the French Revolution. Sir Hopetoun Gabriel Stokes (1873-1951), a high-ranking administrator in India, lived here for the last 15 years of his life. The novelist and journalist Arthur Locker (1828-1893) lived at **No.5** in the 1880s when he was editor of the illustrated newspaper *The Graphic*. The publisher Walter Neurath (1903-67) lived and died at **No.6**. He had escaped from his native Austria upon the Nazi occupation and after the war founded Thames & Hudson. **No.7**

was home to Walter Kenney Jealous, the editor of the *Hampstead & Highgate Express*, until his death here in 1932. He was also president of the Highgate Thirty Club, a debating group which met weekly at the Flask and practised the custom of Swearing on the Horns (p 21).

Nos.8-11, which face west, were built slightly later, and first occupied in 1817. At **No.9** from 1903 until his death in 1940 lived the Dutch decorative painter, Hubert van Hooydonk. In 1972 his widow left her reminiscences to the HLSI. No.11 – now called **No.9A Holly Lodge Gardens** – was used as staff quarters for the Coutts estate, which encompassed all the houses in Holly Terrace as well as houses on the south side of Highgate West Hill (Coutts having acquired the Cooke family lands). The houses were sold off individually when the Coutts estate was broken up in 1922.

Returning to **HIGHGATE WEST HILL**, and turning left soon cross over Holly Lodge Gardens (p 102) and walk down another 50 metres. The long leafy stretch on the opposite side was first developed in the 1830s with four large villas each set in expansive grounds. Only one of these (Westfield, p 81) remains. Alongside the road was a small building and offices, leased in 1831, which the 1840 Southampton estate sale papers record was then being used as a lodge for the Coutts estate (on the east side). It was later known as West Hill Cottage and occupied in the

1860s by Joseph Payne, known as "old Jonathan", a popular judge and supporter of the Ragged School cause; his funeral in 1870 attracted huge crowds. In the 20th century the house became The Bungalow, No.33A, and served as a base for MI6 surveillance of the Soviets, whose Trade Delegation was based behind in The Eagles (p 81). In 1971 more than 100 officials at the Delegation were expelled, accused of spying. The house was recently demolished; in 2007 a luxury house, with three roof terraces, its design inspired by Frank Lloyd Wright, was arising on the rather cramped site.

We cross carefully (avoiding traffic) to the entrance to **No.34**, Hill Court. Walk up to the gates for a view of this imposing structure built in the late 1970s. It lies on the site of one of the four villas, West Hill Place, built in 1833 by the architect Henry Bassett for his brother George, land agent to Lord Southampton. From 1851 the judge Sir William Henry Bodkin (1791-1874), a prolific writer on criminal law, lived here until his death. He was for many years the president of the Society of Arts, of which he was one of the earliest and most enthusiastic members. His only son William Peter Bodkin moved into the house after he died. In 1920 it was taken over by a Catholic institution for unmarried mothers, officially called Saints Pelagius and Joseph's Home for Penitent Women, although usually referred to as St Pelagia's

ROUTE **4**

Home. (Pelagia was a courtesan who, after baptism, wore the garb of a male penitent and called herself Pelagius.) The home was run by the Sisters of the Sacred Heart of Jesus and Mary, who had a convent here. The girls, many from Ireland, slept four to each dormitory and were put to work in a laundry on the site. Some of their babies were taken back to Ireland for adoption from the sister convent in County Cork. The home was closed in 1972 and the buildings were sold for development.

Return up the hill on this west side and pass a very weather-worn early-19th-century stone marker post in the pavement. This gave the distance to the City. It was hit by a car in 1998 and kept safe by local residents until the Council agreed to re-erect it in 2001.

We now reach **MERTON LANE**, where we turn left. Before the 1830s this was simply a right of way to Hampstead. In 1838 Charles Fitzroy, 3rd Baron Southampton, had the meandering footpath straightened and shortly afterwards widened to form the road. The name came from Merton Lodge (p 75), which Meaburn Tatham had built on a 2-acre site at the foot of the hill, leased from Lord Southampton in the same year. During the 19th century this was one of only four houses in large grounds that fronted the road, which retained a gravel surface until the housing developments of the 1970s.

The first two houses opposite on our right were built in the late 1930s in the grounds of Highgate Lodge. **Merton House** and the larger **Highgate House** (No.2) are both in a late-17th-century style; the first owner of the latter called it Wilmary House, after the monarchs William and Mary. William Brittain, the editor of *The Recorder*, was living in Highgate House in 1953 when he lost a libel action brought against him by Canon Lewis Collins whom the paper had branded a communist.

On the left-hand side we walk alongside the surviving wall and 19th-century lodge of Mayfield, the northernmost of the four villas built along Highgate West Hill. It dated from 1833. On the 1862 Stanford map it is marked as Carlton House; it was then home to the stockbroker John Scrimgeour, whose son Walter later bought Parkfield (p 68). After WWII Mayfield housed the St Joseph's Maternity Hospital, part of St Pelagia's Home, but in 1972 the building was demolished and replaced by the development called **WEST HILL PARK**.

This gated, luxury estate was constructed in 1972-78 by Ted Levy, Benjamin & Partners. The Soviet Trade Delegation objected to its construction on the basis that it would be an invasion of privacy and could reduce the value of its own property. The Camden Planning Committee Chairman, Ivor Walker, recorded the Committee's surprise "that a socialist organisation should express their views in such capitalist terms". The 52 brick-built houses, with pantiled sloping roofs, are set among landscaped grounds. At **No.35** the Nigerian politician, Joseph Sarwuan Tarka, died in 1980, aged 50. He had been a leader of the 2-million-strong Tiv people.

We soon cross over the first entrance to West Hill Park (leading to **Nos.1-21**). Note the plaques in ancient Mexican style; the developers were called Aztec Properties. The entrance lies over the site of a Victorian villa called Green Bank. This was built in the grounds of West Hill Place in 1859 to house William Peter Bodkin JP (1814-1900), who lived here until his father died. He had eight children, and born here was the youngest, the criminal lawyer Sir Archibald Henry Bodkin (1862-1957). Sir Archibald's greatest murder prosecution (1915) was that of the serial bigamist George Joseph Smith, perpetrator of the notorious 'Brides in the Bath Murders'; during the trial Bodkin called 112 witnesses for the Crown. In the 1920s he was Director of Public Prosecutions. Green Bank was home from 1886 to 1902 to the Secretary of the HLSI, John Lloyd, who published *The History, Topography and Antiquities of Highgate* while living here. The physician Dr Daniel Eli Anderson was here from 1908, but in 1920 the house was taken over by St Pelagia's Home.

Opposite, just past detached 1930s Heath Winds, is the entrance to private **Heathfield Park**. It contains just one house of the same name, lying on the site of Littleholt, which had been built in 1928 when it was noted for all its mod cons. Littleholt was pulled down in the late 1990s and replaced by a large house with a curved frontage, semi-circular in plan, with a central dome, designed by Alan Power who has also worked at The Elms (p 66). It lies unseen at the end of the road that was laid out over part of the Southampton Lodge estate (p 64), which extended to this middle section of **MERTON LANE**. Also built on the land was detached **No.5**, set well back at the end of a long driveway. It looks older but it too dates from the late 1920s and was first known as Windy Gap. Then it was home to Sir F W Andrewes (p 53) who died here in 1932. Cross over for a slightly closer view.

As the road begins to dip more steeply we pass 19th-century stuccoed **Holly Court Lodge**. Holly Court itself was originally Merton Lodge, erected in 1839 and built by the solicitor Meaburn Tatham, Director of Legal & General Life Assurance Society, founded 3 years before. His second son attended Merton College, Oxford, which may explain the house's name. Tatham lived here until his death in 1875. It was then home to Sir John Glover before his move to nearby Highgate Lodge. The house was renamed Holly Court when William Pearson, chemical manufacturer, lived here. In October 1927 it became an Open Air School run by the LCC for 'delicate' children, i.e. those who were held back

educationally by illness and/or poverty. It closed in 1939 and during WWII the school was used as a fire station; the house was badly bombed, but rebuilt after the war. In 1960 new buildings replaced the old, and Holly Court School was opened for slow learners and backward children. It was altered again in 1981 when it became an ILEA special school, handed over to Camden in 1990. Permission to demolish it was given in 1993 and within three years it had been replaced by an enclave of seven luxury houses.

Opposite is the second entrance to West Hill Park (Nos.22-42). We continue down the hill on the pavement on the right-hand side and pass gated **HAVERSHAM PLACE**, whose seven houses cover the site of the school and sit in well landscaped grounds. Haversham is a Buckinghamshire village near Milton Keynes; or perhaps a Dickensian connection was intended.

Cross **MERTON LANE** near the bottom by the entrance to Nos.23&25. **No.23**, built 1969-71 by Robert Howard, has two wings linked by a spiral staircase. It is all in brick, but with a wood-panelled frontage overlooking Hampstead Heath.

We have now joined **MILLFIELD LANE** (see also p 60). Turn left and cross to the other side. We walk alongside Hampstead Heath with a fine view over the **Model Boating Pond**. A Highgate Model Yacht Club was formed in 1850. It had nautical rules, and officers with pompous

titles such as Commodore. The architect Lewis Vulliamy had a boat called *Lady of The Lake*, and he and two members of his family competed here for a silver cup. The club held races here until WWI and only disbanded shortly before 1980.

The Mill Field is mentioned in a survey, undertaken in the reign of Henry VIII, of Kenwood, from which it lay south east. The whereabouts of the eponymous mill are unknown; it was not mentioned in the survey and may have already disappeared. No trace of it survives on maps or in field names, although some hold that a windmill may have been on Parliament Hill. However, the road was called *Milford* Lane in the later 18th century (a map of 1761; a letter to the Fitzroys from the parish clerk in 1800; rate books before 1808), which suggests that the mill was on the Highgate arm of the River Fleet which runs through today's ponds. There were many watermills along the course of the Fleet in the Middle Ages.

As we continue, look left at the 20th-century buildings facing us; set well back above the road are houses in West Hill Park. There follows, at **No.44**, a rather forbidding, and dull, modernist office block, behind a security fence. It now houses the Office of the Defence Attaché of the Russian Federation. It was built by Eric Lyons in 1957 for the Soviet Trade Delegation (p 81), after the Government overruled objections by St Pancras Council. The 5-storey block was built in what had been the grounds of The Eagles (p 81) that had stretched to Millfield Lane; it lies over a lodge and gardener's cottage built in the 1840s.

Beyond, standing on a rise, is **No.40**, Hill House, in an 18th-century style with canted bays and a brick parapet. The bricks look old, but this building dates from just before WWII. It was called Woldmere until 1952. It was recently converted from three self-contained flats into a large single dwelling house. This and the next two houses were all built on what had been the lower grounds of Westfield (p 81). **No.38**, also set well back from the road, is in a low-slung, Scandinavian style by Pank Goss Associates, 1968-9. Behind a high fence you can make out the glazed gable of **No.36**, dating from the same period. This was the home of the diplomat Sir Michael Alexander (1936-2002), who was assistant private secretary to Margaret Thatcher in her first three years as prime minister. He also fenced and won a silver medal at the Rome Olympics in 1960. He died here of cancer in June 2002.

Next door, and again behind a high fence, make out the sharply pointed brick gable of **No.34**. No.32 is lost behind greenery. It dates from the 1940s and is called **White House Cottage**, taking its name from the large house at No.2 Millfield Place, whose grounds originally stretched here.

No.30, Pond House, is a large detached villa with prominent striped awnings, set a long way back from the road. It stands on the site of a villa erected in 1842 and known as Whittlebury Cottage during the 20-year occupation of Charles Stevens (d.1867), Secretary of the County Fire Office. That house was rebuilt in 1870, becoming known as Millfield until it was renamed Waratah in 1905, when it was owned by the Foy family, who ran a furniture business in Sydney. They had the house rebuilt again, in colonial style, during WWI: this is the villa we see now. Norman Shand Kydd (d.1962) married Frances Foy in 1920 and moved in, living at the house for over a decade. Their son Peter Shand Kydd (1925-2006) was born here. Later in life Peter sold the family wallpaper business to try his hand at sheep farming in Australia, but he returned to England to marry the mother of Diana, Princess of Wales. Edith Summerskill (1901-80) lived at No.30, by then Pond House, from 1951 until her death. A feminist from girlhood, she was a fiery political speaker, popular in the Labour Party, although she never achieved very high office. When she entered the Lords she championed causes dear to her, such as women's rights, abortion law reform and the abolition of boxing. Her husband, the physician Dr Jeffrey Samuel, with whom she had run a long-standing joint medical practice before WWII, sold the house in 1982.

On the west side we pass another entrance to the Heath, with the steep embankment protecting the **Highgate Men's Bathing Pond** clearly visible. Swimming has long been popular in the ponds, although this was private land before 1889. The pond opened to the public on 1 May 1893 with no fanfare, but was popularised through the efforts of Robert Sandon, later an Olympic swimmer and a president of the swimming and diving-club, the Highgate Life-buoys, who have been based here since their formation in 1903. Among the many races they have organised is an invigorating (or foolhardy) race on Christmas Day. The clubhouse burned down in 1997 and their records and photographs were destroyed. From 1902 exclusive use of the pool was given to ladies on Wednesdays until their own pool further north was opened. In the earlier 20th century the men's pond was much used for diving – Olympic hopefuls trained here – but the 10-metre board was removed in 1980 as the water had become too shallow. In recent years male nude sunbathing, which had been tolerated for many years despite a 1909 Heath regulation, has been a cause of some controversy. It is now officially sanctioned but only in one section of the concreted changing compound, which since 1994 has been divided in two by a 'privacy screen'. In 2005 the Corporation of London introduced a (voluntary) fee to use the ponds, which had previously been free of charge.

Facing the pond is Grade-II-Listed Kenwood Cottage at **No.24**, pantiled, and hung with wisteria. There was a building here from at least the 18th century; except for Millfield Cottage (see below), it was the only dwelling shown along present Millfield Lane on the map of 1804. At that time it was called Millfield Farm, and for a number of years from 1809 ratebooks record the road as Millfield Farm Lane. The house was then owned by Henry Coxwell (not the balloonist), who had an orchard on the Heath side of the lane, and a few outbuildings, including a laboratory where he conducted chemical experiments; he was chairman of the Committee of Chymistry at the Society of Arts. Coxwell was at Millfield Farm until the early 1830s. The 1834 map shows the building as Old Millfield Farm, although by then it was more often known as Millfield House. The freehold of the land was granted in 1833 to Miss Lucy Gason and she was still here 40 years later. Two early-19th-century pictures at Guildhall show the house as a 3-bayed, 3-storey, stuccoed building, and when the house was sold in 1879 it was described as having 10 beds, stabling and a coach house with pleasure ground. Its grounds were incorporated into Millfield (present No.30) behind, and the house was demolished in 1881, its coach house and stables being retained and the rateable value halving. On the 1881 census a herdsman is living in 'Millfield House', but the remaining buildings were soon after being used as a coachhouse for employees of the owners of No.2 Southampton Villas (p 79). In the 20th century after Millfield was renamed Waratah, this building was known for a time as Waratah Cottage, but by WWII it had assumed its present name. The building was extended in 1989-90 by the architects Henry Osborne Christmas Associates, whose sign can be seen on the wall they added, in old bricks surrounding a thermal window.

On the west side in the 19th century was a handful of cottages housing laundresses and labourers, which overlooked the ponds, including one called appropriately Pond Cottage. This was set back and had a view of **Highgate No.1 Pond**, not visible from the road. These buildings were swept away in the 1880s, before Highgate Men's Bathing Pond was in use as such.

On the right, as the road turns sharp left, is the large Grade-II-Listed **Millfield Cottage**, with a steeply pitched roof and prominent chimneys. It has changed drastically over the centuries. It was remodelled in the early 1920s in an antique fashion by Arthur and Charles Burckhardt, who ran a firm of estate agents at No.110 Highgate West Hill before WWII. It probably incorporates two separate buildings. One was once the residence of employees of the Hampstead Waterworks Company; the deeds date back to 1693, but it may well be earlier in origin. It was called the Water House until 1807, but the following year ratebooks show a residential building here which was double the value. Turncocks continued to live alongside until the 1850s, when the company became incorporated into the New River Company. One, called James Dobbins, came home on 26 October 1814 to find Elizabeth, his common-law wife, gruesomely beaten to death with a poker, left at the scene. A witness at the trial said he was at work at "Mr Whitehead's", not 25 yards from Dobbins' cottage. This was probably the large house built in 1808 which became known as Millfield Cottage. By 1816 it was owned by Charles Toussaint, who went bankrupt a few years later; at the subsequent sale in 1822 it was described as "very genteel" and "substantial", with 7 bedrooms and outbuildings. There is an unproven tradition that John Ruskin spent part of his childhood here.

By the bend is **No.16**, dating from about 1960. Attached to it is a small 3-bed property known as **The Studio**. Squeezed in between two blank walls, it was designed by Doug Clelland, who won a RIBA award upon its completion in 1993. It was constructed of largely untreated natural materials, with a large oriel window to let in light. Cross over to its gate for a closer view. Ben Weinreb (1912-99) had a hand in its design. He lived at No.16 for two decades from 1970 with his second wife Joan.

He was a renowned architectural book and print seller, with a shop at 93 Great Russell Street, and compiled *The London Encyclopaedia* with Christopher Hibbert.

All the buildings on the side opposite No.16 lie over Brookfield, a meadow through which the Highgate arm of the River Fleet drained down from the ponds. The edge of the meadow began to be built over during the Regency period. At that time Brookfield was often considered part of Kentish Town, which had not yet become an undesirable address. Indeed, Highgate West Hill was then sometimes called Kentish Town Hill.

The 'moderne' flats that are **West Hill Court** stand on the site of Ivy Cottage, the home of the 19th-century comedian and actor Charles Mathews (1776–1835) [20]. He was famous for his 'At Homes', comprising a monologue full of jest and anecdote that carried his audience through a series of amusing adventures, and a farce, in which he played multiple characters using his skills in quick changes and ventriloquy. Londoners and people from the provinces flocked to the West End to see them each year. He undertook a triumphant tour of America in 1822 and returned to England as *the* comedian of the age. Charles Dickens claimed that he always went to see him when he played, and Mathews inspired the character of Alfred Jingle in *The Pickwick Papers*. He was forever joking; on his deathbed he

20 Actor Charles Mathews, painted by James Lonsdale; mezzotint engraving by C Turner (Heal Collection)

was mistakenly given some ink instead of medicine and told the doctor not to worry, asking him for some blotting paper to swallow. Mathews called his pleasant thatched cottage, which was built in 1819, his "Tusculum". It was adorned externally with trellis work wreathed and overgrown with jasmine and honeysuckle. In it several

rooms were devoted to his theatrical picture-gallery, which the Garrick Club acquired after his death.

The next occupant was James Shoolbred of furniture store fame, who enlarged the house in 1833; an 1841 sale notice stated that £7,000 had been spent on it and that the neighbourhood "is now considered infinitely the most Distingué". By the 1860s when the wealthy solicitor William Ford, a governor of Highgate School, was living here the building was too grand to be called a cottage and was renamed Brookfield House. A letter in the Heal Collection shows that in 1889 Ambrose Heal himself was thinking of buying the property; it then had 16 bedrooms, and piggeries in the grounds. A later resident, politician Thomas McKinnon Wood (1855-1927), lived here when he was leader of the Progressive party on the LCC. He was later elected as a Liberal MP, becoming Secretary of State for Scotland in 1912. In 1915 Brookfield House became the Queen Alexandra Hospital for Officers. It was pulled down in 1934.

The flats called West Hill Court were then erected. Contemporary advertisements promised "sunlight in every room". The flats were bombed in WWII and several had to wait until 1946 to be repaired. Residents have included Thomas, Baron Brimelow (1915-95), head of the diplomatic service 1973-75 and an acknowledged authority on Soviet affairs. In 1971, as deputy under-secretary of state, Brimelow advised the mass expulsion of Soviet intelligence agents. On retirement, he served for two years as an MEP. He died at No.12. The writer, poet, songwriter and broadcaster Alasdair Clayre (1935-84) lived at No.38 during the 1970s.

Beyond West Hill Court is stuccoed Fern Lodge at **No.5**, amidst greenery. It dates from 1822. 25-year-old Henry Rose stole six tame rabbits from the Bullock family who were living here in 1830 and was transported for the crime. The publisher Eliot Stock moved here from Aller Cottage (p 85) in 1870 and was in residence until 1911. After WWII it was home to Ambrose Appelbe before his move to The Elms (p 66). The next occupant was the Lithuanian-born sociologist and philosopher Morris Ginsberg (1889–1970), who lived here for some 20 years until his death. He was long associated with the London School of Economics, where he held the chair of sociology from 1929. Next door is little **Cameo Lodge**, a small brick house painted white and lying obliquely to the road; it was once the coachman's cottage of No.14 Highgate West Hill, the large house on the corner ahead.

On the north side of the road is tall **No.12**, Millbrook (otherwise Millbrook House), with adjoining coach house, a grand stuccoed villa built in 1844 for the solicitor William Ford. It was later owned by members of the extensive Highgate family, the Tathams. In the 1890s this and nearby Millfield housed the Craven College for Boys. Dr Grace Watson ran a nursing home here during WWII but sold the house in 1944, and it became the Homerton College Hostel until 1963. Alongside it was once a similar villa called The Laurels in large grounds, built in 1843 by Edward Henry Browne for Albert Walls. From 1951 this housed Syskon College but by 1973 The Laurels had given way to the present terrace of four neo-Georgian town houses (**Nos.4-10**). The name of the college lives on at Syskon Cottage, **No.2**.

Near the end of the road turn left up private and rather steep **MILLFIELD PLACE**, where three houses enjoying views over the ponds were built in the early years of Queen Victoria's reign. The two nearest the top were substantial and were known as Southampton Villas; the road was named only in 1943. **No.1**, built in 1844 but reconstructed a century later, was the home of the timber merchant Bignell George Elliott, from 1892 to 1905. The first occupant of **No.2** (built in 1842 as No.2 Southampton Villas), was the bookseller Joseph Johnson Miles; his widow was still living here until her death in 1908. The next occupant, Jacob de Graaf, named the house Insulinde, presumably because he was connected with the Sumatran rubber plantation and company of that name. After WWII it was called the White House, where the composer and pianist Sir Clifford Curzon (1907-82) lived from 1955 up to his death. It is now Grade-II-Listed. The largest house, **No.3** (once No.1 Southampton Villas) was built in 1839. Living here from 1865 to 1868 was Frederick Lloyd, manager of Richard Lloyd Ltd who made Old Holborn tobacco. In the early 20th century the house was renamed Leskinfere. Its former coachhouse, at the end of the lane, is now **No.3A**. From here there is a good view over London, towards the southern heights.

Return to Millfield Lane, and turn left to meet **HIGHGATE WEST HILL**. Cross carefully to the other side and walk uphill as far as the second bench, where you may care to rest. The houses on this east side all form part of the interwar Holly Lodge Estate (see Route 6) but the houses opposite at Nos.15-26 were built in the late 1850s. Until 1893 they were called Hermitage Villas. The first four are terraced; the rest are semi-detached. **No.15** was home from 1928 for some 20 years to Sophie Ritchie, one of the earliest female magistrates. At **No.19** from 1891 to 1894 lived the journalist (William) Algernon Locker (1863-1930), editor of the *Morning Post* and the *Irish Times* and a contributor to *Punch*. His father, the novelist and journalist Arthur Locker died here in June 1893. **No.23** was home for nearly three decades from 1892 to William Blair, surveyor and engineer for St Pancras.

A prep school run by Miss Esther Garman was based at **No.24** from 1875 to 1889. **No.26** was the home until WWII of the novelist Martha Garnett (1869-1946) and her solicitor husband Robert. Martha was a leading light in the Highgate branch of the Central Society for Women's Suffrage, alongside Mrs Harrington of Holly Terrace.

Hermitage Villas replaced a group of copyhold cottages called Slater's Rents that were built shortly before 1800 on a strip enclosed from the waste (or common) in the 17th century. John Slater was living here until his death in 1808; his widow Elizabeth was the ratepayer until 1815 when the buildings were taken over by George Charles Smith; they are shown as Smith's Cottages on census returns. The largest of the group was at No.8. Called The Hermitage, it was leased by Mary Howitt (p 72) from Spring 1853, while her husband William was prospecting for gold in Australia. Its site is the garden of present No.26. The Hermitage was enclosed by tall trees and adjoined a smaller and much older tenement which the Howitts asserted was the "real and original Hermitage". The Howitts [21] wrote that one of its tenants had been the dandy Walsh Porter, decorative consultant to the Prince Regent, who used to come to gamble and drink

21 William and Mary Howitt at The Hermitage (*Good Words*, March 1886)

here. The ceilings were supposedly painted with naked figures, and, swathed in ivy, the building could conceal many an orgy. The Howitts claimed that Porter shot himself dead there (he was heavily in debt at the time). They also alleged that before his trial and execution the notorious forger Henry Fauntleroy (1784-1824) concealed himself at the Hermitage.

The five houses beyond at Nos.27-31, with their gables facing the road, date from 1860 when they replaced a group of four cottages built in the early 1830s as part of Slater's Rents. In one of the latter, Ivy Cottage, the by then impoverished artist Henry Thomas Alken died shortly after appearing on the 1851 census. He had been the dominant sporting artist of the day, and well in with the wealthy young set who gathered at Melton Mowbray to hunt, drink and (on at least one occasion literally) paint the town red. Richard Whitmore, principal clerk in the Customs House, was the first inhabitant of Mortimer Cottage (**No.29**) from 1860. He was also librarian at the HLSI. **No.31** was the childhood home of John Betjeman. The blue plaque, placed here in September 2006, states that his family lived in the house from 1908 until 1917. In his 1960 blank verse autobiography *Summoned by Bells* Betjeman fondly remembers the house (*deeply I loved thee, 31 West Hill*) and recalls his first childhood love, Peggy Purey-Cust, the daughter of the owner of No.82:

Satchel on back I hurried up West Hill
To catch you on your morning walk to school
Your nanny with you and your golden hair
Streaming like sunlight.

The writer Iain Hamilton was living at No.31 when he wrote a review of *Summoned by Bells*, and his mother died at the house in 1967.

North of this point as far as Merton Lane four grand villas, each in large grounds running down towards the ponds, were erected in the 1830s. The two to the north – Mayfield and West Hill Place – we described earlier. Below them was The Eagles (former No.33), which was built in 1834 for Thomas Clarke, a solicitor in Ordnance who died at the house in 1854. A few years later the wholesale druggist Robert Barclay lived there, followed in the 1880s by Alfred Goslett JP (d.1886), who had founded a plate glass and ironmongery firm and after whom Goslett Yard off Charing Cross Road is named. In 1896 The Eagles became the home of Daniel Collard, the piano manufacturer and in the interwar period of Alfred Davies, the Conservative MP for Lincoln. The southernmost villa, **Westfield**, built in 1837, survives unseen behind the trees ahead. Westfield's first owner was the barrister John Tatham, and the house remained in his family's possession until 1898; it was then taken over by Charles Turner, chaplain to Queen Victoria who had just been created the first and only Bishop of Islington. He had no official residence, so he bought Westfield. Just after WWI the shipowner Michael Embiricos was living here, when he purchased Southampton Lodge (p 64). John Cadman, first Baron Cadman (1877-1941), mining engineer and industrialist, lived at Westfield in the 1920s, having become the leading British authority on oil during WWI. In 1923 Cadman became the managing director of the Anglo-Persian Oil Company, and in 1927 its chairman, a post he retained until his death. The house was modernised in the early 1930s, but in 1936 its owner proposed to demolish it to make way for four blocks of flats. Local protests thwarted this. A year later the Russian Club and School moved in and the Soviet Trade Delegation took over The Eagles. The latter was finally demolished in 1967 after planning permission had been given for a 4-storey modernist office block, designed by Dinerman, Davison and Hillman and completed in 1969; the design won a Civic Trust award in 1971. The block is now **Nos.32&33**. The entrance to the grounds of the Soviet delegation's successor body (the Trade Delegation of the Russian Federation) is flanked by the old lodge to Westfield.

Now retrace your steps to Millfield Lane but continue down Highgate West Hill on the eastern side, looking at the properties opposite. The line of houses below Millfield Lane was built at the edge

of Brookfield on land leased from the Fitzroys between 1814 and 1820; most date from that period. By the early 1830s they were listed as Nos.1-10 Highgate Rise, a name retained until 1893.

Grade-II-Listed **No.14** on the corner is a large stuccoed villa, visible in an 1822 view **[22]** of the Highgate No.1 Pond. Its grounds were leased for building in 1814 and it appears in ratebooks two years later. Usually called Millfield Villa in the 19th century, it was known simply as Millfield when, from 1905, it was home to Thomas H W Idris, founder of the once famous soft-drinks company and Liberal MP for Flint Burghs in 1906-1910. After he moved out in 1913, William Shand Kydd, founder of the eponymous wallpaper firm, lived here until his death in 1936. After WWII it housed the St Pancras Female Orphanage, subsequently Millfield Children's Home. This was run by the St Pancras Foundation, which had to close the home in 2002, unable to raise the cash needed to bring it up to Government standards. Now known as Millfield House, the building was converted into flats in 2006. Just beyond its (restored) garden wall is a marker post inscribed "III½ miles to St Giles Pound".

22 'View from the ponds at the foot of Highgate Hill, drawn from Nature' in 1822 by T. M. Baynes" (Wallis Bequest). From left to right: Millfield Cottage; Ivy Lodge; Fern Cottage; and Millfield Villa.

There follows a succession of houses dating mainly from the 1820s, mostly Listed Grade II, and all sited well above the roadway. The first are semi-detached Nos.12&13: **No.13** boasts an excellent Georgian style fanlight, while **No.12** has a small wooden veranda above the doorway. Nos.10&11, another early-19th-century pair of stuccoed semis, are shielded by trees. The four properties were developed by the lawyer Ferdinando Jeyes, who lived at **No.10**, before suffering a fatal heart attack at Drury Lane Theatre in 1843. The same house was home from 1870 until his death of William Longman (1813-77) of the famous publishing family. (In 1890, Longmans were to buy out the Rivington firm, which also had Highgate connections.) At **No.11** lived the merchant Richard Carter Smith, the first Secretary of the HLSI until 1849, when he was ordained. Thomas Smith, solicitor of Furnival's Inn, was then here for nearly 50 years, and his son Vernon Russell Smith KC (1849-1921), later a prominent Chancery lawyer, was born at the house. In 1912 Algernon Locker moved here from No.19.

The present **No.9**, beyond, was built shortly before WWII, replacing a villa that had been pulled down in 1927. This had been home for well over 70 years to a school run successively by Professor Louis Sumond from Hanover, his English wife and his nephew Carl Schroeder. It specialised in teaching French and German

to its dozen or so female pupils.

On the east side we reach the entrance to Grade-II-Listed **St Anne's Brookfield**. Walk along the curving driveway for a closer look. This sweeps past a lawn with a war memorial. The church was erected in 1853 by Miss Anne Barnett in memory of her brother Richard who died two years before. Together they had tried to build the church in 1841 but had failed to raise sufficient funds to buy the land from its owner, Harry Chester; he later gave Anne the site. The church was designed in Decorated style by George Plunkett, a partner in the firm of Cubitt, and has a fine tower and stone spire. The bells were presented by Miss Burdett-Coutts. Their peal inspired the title of Betjeman's *Summoned by Bells*; they provide the only proper ring in Highgate. St Anne's became a separate parish in 1868. The church was refurbished in 1978.

The vicarage lay just beyond, set in large grounds which were taken for **ST ANNE'S CLOSE**, a gated development of houses built in 1950-52 to the plans of Walter Segal, for himself and friends. Walk in to see the 2-storey houses, set on unfenced lawns and grouped around a communal garden, on your left. The far side of the garden affords an interesting back view of St Anne's church and its serried ranks of roofs. Return to the entrance of the Close. Here, on your right, is **No.106 HIGHGATE WEST HILL**, the present Vicarage, while to the left is the former Vicarage, **Brookfield Lodge**, Nos.107-108.

This house (now divided into two) is on the site of the Cow and Hare inn that is mentioned in 1704 court rolls, but which disappears from licensing records after 1721. It was leased the following year by Thomas Phillips, inn-holder of Highgate, along with 50 acres and the White Hart (p 69). By 1770 the Cow and Hare had been replaced by a farmhouse, occupied by the farmer Thomas Greenwood from 1770 until 1815. Harriot Coutts then acquired the land. By 1827 the farmland had become gardens, and the cottage was leased to Giles Redmayne, mercer. The house features prominently in the memoirs of his son Robert Robey Redmayne (1828-1907), now in the British Library. When Giles left in 1837, it was demolished and the land was sold to Richard Barnett, a director of Meux's brewery, who lived opposite at No.6. He built the present Nos.107-108, in grey brick with broad eaves, before his death in 1851. Anne Barnett (d.1858) bequeathed the house as a vicarage for the church she had built.

Across the road to our right more early-19th-century houses survive. **No.8** is a detached small villa in which the publisher George Rivington (1801-58), brother and partner of Francis (p 71) was living in the 1830s. It was later home to the Wesleyan Methodist minister William Maclardie Bunting (1805-66), who died here. A selection of his sermons, letters, poems and hymns was published posthumously by his younger brother. **Nos.6&7** are stuccoed semis. The service road by the side of No.6 leads behind the flats of Brookfield to diminutive Mulberry Cottage. It is marked **No.5**, although that is officially the address of the whole Estate of which it forms a part.

A detached villa called Brookfield, fronting the field of the same name, was erected in 1816 by Joseph Gardiner. It had extensive grounds. The lawyer Nathaniel Basevi lived here in the 1830s before moving to Beechwood (p 54). Brookfield became No.1 Highgate Rise and subsequently No.5 West Hill. The solicitor Charles Hyde, Secretary of the London Fever Hospital, lived here in the 1840s and 1850s. The last occupant was Charles Matthews, later mayor of St Pancras, who was still living in the house in 1901. The following year the mansion flats that now cover the site were constructed. These are also called **Brookfield** (otherwise Brookfield Mansions). Matthews began the first block, to the south of his house, a couple of years earlier. Two identical tall blocks – Nos.17-24 (on the site of the villa) and Nos.9-16 – front the road, before the entrance with its caretaker's lodge. Cross the road carefully to reach the lodge and walk in. A narrow bush-lined path winds its way to the long block Nos.25-56, following the line of the River Fleet. The Estate is very peaceful, with beautifully tended gardens.

An early resident of a Brookfield flat was the then journalist, Edmund Clerihew Bentley, whose elder son was born here in 1903. Bentley's middle name will always be remembered in the English language as a literary form. Thomas Idris lived at No.13 in the early 1920s. No.25 was home in the late 1940s to another journalist, John Connell (the alias of John Henry Robertson), who achieved fame as a biographer and writer on politics. He founded the Noise Abatement Society. Charles Matthews himself lived at No.26 before his death in Jamaica in 1930. No.30 was home to the actor and playwright Arnold Ridley (1896-1984), author of the play *The Ghost Train* but best remembered as Private Godfrey in the TV series *Dad's Army*. Sir Sydney Olivier (1859-1943), a noted Fabian who had served as Governor of Jamaica, was living at No.37 just after WWI. Ramsay Macdonald made him Secretary of State for India. He was the uncle of the actor Laurence Olivier. The architect Sir John Simpson (1858–1933), president of RIBA from 1919 to 1921, died at his home, No.39. He specialised in the design of public buildings and schools, including Roedean near his native Brighton. He is best known for his work at the British Empire Exhibition which was held at Wembley in 1924, where, in collaboration with his partner Maxwell Ayrton, he was responsible for the general layout and for the (now demolished) stadium. Henry Durant, the head of Gallup Polls UK and who popularised opinion polls, lived at No.53 from 1955 to 1982. No.56 was home to Eric Fenby (1906-97), amanuensis of the composer Delius and later Professor of Music at the Royal College of Music. The actress Elisabeth Bergner (1897-1986), who was said to have been the inspiration for the character of Margo Channing in the film *All About Eve*, spent her last years at Brookfield.

Return to Highgate West Hill and turn right. Although there is nothing today above ground to announce it, we have crossed the Highgate arm of the River Fleet and left behind the estate of the Fitzroys, although we are still at the edge of the former meadow called Brookfield. In the early 19th century the river was 13ft wide at this point.

Opposite is a collection of garages and a low brick block with shops, turning the corner into Swain's Lane (pp 42, 109). These were built on the edge of the gardens of St Anne's Vicarage. **No.110** was once the estate agents run by Arthur and Charles Burckhardt (p 77) between the wars. Thompson's map of 1804 shows a large pond here, formed by the Fleet.

Past Nos.1-4a Brookfield is a slightly earlier block (1893) in similar style and incorporating at ground-floor level the commercial premises at **Nos.1-4**. Note the fine rubbed brickwork, the egg-and-dart

moulding course and the line of Greek fretwork. The block was built on the site of two early-19th-century cottages, Meadow Cottage and Aller Cottage. The latter was presumably named by Charles Hyde of former No.5, who died in 1859 at Aller (Somerset), where he owned property. Between 1868 and 1870 Aller Cottage was home to the publisher Eliot Stock; and then, from 1873 to 1879, to impresario Richard D'Oyly Carte, the producer of Gilbert and Sullivan operas.

On the side of No.1 we can make out old painted signs advertising refreshments. This has long been a café. In the 1920s the proprietor, L Vaccarossa, declared: "whenever you want a real meal come to me!" On its rear wall a sign announces: "caterers for beanfeasts". It stands on a corner of Parliament Hill Fields, called Dukes Field, which has been public open space since 1889, but for much of the 19th century was occupied by nursery gardens. Along the footpath to our right stands modern, detached **No.**1A, Meadow Lodge, a park keeper's residence.

Beyond No.1 is a selection of bus stops from which buses can be taken back to Highgate village or to several other destinations.

Highgate New Town
Downhill walk from Highgate Hill to Swain's Lane
For modern map see back cover

Highgate's healthful reputation attracted to its lower slopes several hospitals, built by the Victorians for the treatment of the urban poor. Some of their present-day successors we encounter in the early part of this walk. We then drop into Highgate New Town, a once far from healthy area that was widely regarded as an insanitary slum. Part redeveloped and part renovated in the 1970s, it is cherished today by its residents and has a strong community spirit.

From the 'Waterlow Park' bus stop on Highgate Hill, walk down to the complex crossroads once known as Suicide Corner (p 44). Intersecting from the right is **DARTMOUTH PARK HILL**, formerly the northern end of Maiden Lane. Here that ancient thoroughfare ended its 3-mile climb from Battle Bridge (King's Cross), having served throughout its length as the parish (and later borough) boundary between St Pancras and Islington. The lane's original name may have derived from an image of the Virgin that stood beside it before the Reformation, or perhaps from the middens or dust heaps it passed. It was sometimes known as Black Dog Lane, after the Old Black Dog tavern, which once

ROUTE **5**

85

stood on the corner site ahead, dominated now by St Joseph's church (p 44). Pre-dating even Highgate Hill, the medieval lane is believed to have continued east from here on the line of Hornsey Lane, to your left. The first and most distinguished Chief Surveyor to the St Pancras Vestry (1856-91), William Scott Booth, described the condition in 1856 of this ancient boundary route: "it was narrow and devious, the many crooks and turns perpetuating the erratic course of the aboriginal footpath through the intricacies of the primeval forest".

Turning right into Dartmouth Park Hill, and rounding a bend, continue downhill, with Waterlow Park on your right. Pass a second park entrance, with its 2-storey former park-keeper's cottage **Dartmouth Park Lodge**. Beyond the modern St Joseph's RC Primary School (left), reach the entrance on the right to the **Highgate Mental Health Centre**, until recently the Highgate Wing of the Whittington Hospital (see below). In 1867 the St Pancras Board of Guardians bought from the Chester estate this 3¾-acre site, a meadow once known as Abbot's Barn Field. The hospital they erected here, intended for the treatment of sick inmates of the parish workhouse, was quickly taken over (1870) by the Central London Sick Asylum District (CLSAD), a new body chaired by Sir Sydney Waterlow. St Pancras Infirmary drew patients from various inner parishes from Bloomsbury to Westminster. Walk a few metres beyond the traffic barrier for a good overview of the site. Designed by Messrs John Giles & Biven, the Infirmary **[23]** comprised a central administrative block, still standing, topped by a squat steeple. This housed the kitchen, laundry, operating theatre and the quarters of the resident surgeon, his assistant and the matron. Here on the east side of the site were three blocks containing the women's wards. Surgical wards for each sex were on the lower (south) side, while two blocks of men's wards stood near the western edge, beyond a house for the hospital's Steward.

Mr Lewis, the Steward, was soon embroiled in an instance of Victorian sleaze. Alfred Baker, the 'gas and water man', sacked by Lewis for alleged idleness, wrote to Sir Sydney accusing his former boss of drunkenness and of mismanaging the hospital's food stores. Lewis in turn blew the whistle on the vice-chairman of the Visiting Committee. The latter, he claimed, had told him (*inter alia*) to charge the £30 cost of a quarter-cask of sherry for the committee's own lavish dinners to the meagre budget intended for patients' wine. The CLSAD upheld Baker's dismissal, and Lewis was encouraged to resign, but no action seems to have been taken against the errant vice-chairman.

The St Pancras Infirmary was, however, praised by Florence Nightingale as the "finest metropolitan hospital". Having been consulted by the architects, she was also instrumental in the appointment of the first matron, Miss Mabel Torrance, who became her close friend. The infirmary's first twelve nurses were trained at Nightingale's own school for nurses at St Thomas's.

The hospital returned in 1883 to the control of the St Pancras Guardians of the Poor, as St Pancras North Infirmary. A plaque in the chapel honours the nurse and national heroine Edith Cavell. Born in 1865, a Suffolk country rector's daughter, she first worked as a governess, taking up nursing only at the age of 30. For two years in 1901-03, Edith served as Night Superintendent of the North Infirmary, often as the only trained nurse on duty and responsible for 500 beds. Later accepting a post in Belgium, she was executed in Brussels in 1915, found guilty by a German court-martial of having helped 200 Allied soldiers to escape to neutral Holland.

In 1930 the LCC took over the Infirmary, which became its 'Highgate Hospital'. In 1949, after the formation of the NHS, it became the Highgate Wing of the Whittington Hospital (see later). Recently refurbished and partly rebuilt, it was reopened in 2005 by Health Secretary Patricia Hewitt as the Highgate Mental Health Centre of the Camden & Islington NHS Mental Health & Social Care Trust. Replacing the unpopular 1980s Waterlow Unit on Highgate Hill, the new centre offers a mostly in-patient service with 136

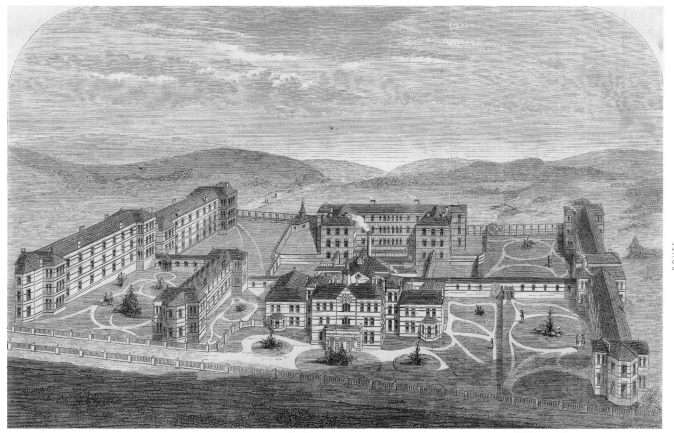

23 St Pancras Infirmary, looking south, with the female wards on the left: architects' drawing (*The Builder*, 9 Jan 1869). The moorland background is a fiction.

beds. Several of the original buildings were retained while others were replaced by new buildings in pale brick, at last providing patients with a room of their own.

Walk on down Dartmouth Park Hill, beside the former female wards, refurbished in 2006 as the administrative offices of the Whittington. Pass the site of the hospital's mortuary, which was built in its southeast corner for ease of access from the road. Pause again.

Opposite, in Islington and extending eastward, are the main precincts of the **Whittington Hospital**. Once standing on the far side, near the foot of Highgate Hill, was the Lazar House of St Anthony, founded in 1473 and closed, with the decline in leprosy, in 1650. Two centuries later, in 1848-50 the Smallpox and Vaccination Hospital, displaced from King's Cross by the new railway terminus, was relocated to a nearby site (behind Dartmouth House flats, just passed). Its grand Italianate building was designed by Samuel Dawkes. Two large workhouse infirmaries were subsequently built in the vicinity. The first was the Holborn and Finsbury Union Infirmary, designed by Henry Saxon Snell & Sons, erected in 1877 on the far side of Highgate Hill at its junction with Archway Road. The second, the Islington Union Infirmary, opened in 1900 on the site directly to your left, the architect being William Smith. Its offices were based in the former

Smallpox and Vaccination Hospital, whose patients moved in the same year to South Mimms. In 1930 the LCC took over these two infirmaries, which became the Archway Hospital and St Mary's Hospital respectively and in 1944 they were grouped administratively with the Highgate Hospital, discussed above. The three hospitals merged formally as the Whittington four years later upon the advent of the NHS. The Smallpox and Vaccination Hospital is now F Wing of Whittington Hospital; the Holborn and Finsbury Union Infirmary has become the Archway Wing; and the Islington Union Infirmary St Mary's Wing. The Whittington was greatly extended in 2006 when a new wing was completed along Magdala Avenue (the next turning on the left).

Whittington is a name much associated with this part of Highgate. Whittington College almshouses, founded in 1424 under the will of the philanthropic Richard Whittington (c.1358-1423) were removed in 1822 from the City to the south end of Archway Road. Near the bottom of Highgate Hill, on the pavement beside the Whittington Stone pub, is the stone itself, dated 1821 but at least the third to be erected there. Now caged, and topped by the figure of a cat added in 1964, it marks the spot where, in legend as in pantomime, 'Dick' Whittington is encouraged to "turn again" on hearing the chimes of Bow Bells. The inscription reads:

Whittington Stone
Sir Richard Whittington
Thrice Lord Mayor of London
1397 Richard II
1406 Henry IV
1420 Henry V
Sheriff in 1393

In fact, Whittington was never knighted, and was Lord Mayor four times. The traditional tale is dubious in another way, in that the "poor boy" apprenticed to a London mercer actually came from a quite affluent Gloucestershire family. The earliest known source of his supposed connection with Highgate was a play, *The History of Richard Whittington*, first performed in 1605, almost two centuries after his death.

Now ahead of you, and to the right, lies Highgate New Town, an area of mostly working-class houses built up between c.1865 and 1882 on the estate of Harry Chester (see p 95), and in multiple occupation from the outset. The earliest houses were on the narrow plateau below, which we reach later. Here in the New Town's northeast corner, two later streets of 2-storey houses climbed the hillside towards our present position, built on the eastern side of a 10-acre meadow known in 1804 as Abbot's Field, and whose western parts became the Eastern Cemetery. Retcar Street descended diagonally southwest to join Raydon Street (p 92), while an L-shaped Lulot Street ran west from here, before turning south to rejoin Retcar Street partway down. On the site just ahead of you, at erstwhile No.193, stood twelve working-class flats once named Model Dwellings, whose original landlord was Samuel Hensby, a Brentwood-born 'carpenter' living in Highgate at No.46 North Road.

By the 1960s the local housing stock needed to be replaced; 75% of households had no bathroom. Comprehensive redevelopment was then in vogue with planners, and central government was demanding the high housing densities associated with high-rise blocks. Sidney Cook (the former Holborn, and by then Camden, Borough Architect) objected to these, favouring high-density low-rise solutions. A joint project with Islington, whose neighbouring streets were in similar need of redevelopment, was begun in 1967, but abandoned a year later when Richard Gibson, the original designer, left Camden.

The **Whittington Estate**, on your right, was Stage 1 of the subsequent redevelopment on the Camden side. Climb the ramp into **LULOT GARDENS**, the uppermost of the Estate's four pedestrian streets. Begun in 1972, they were designed by Peter Tábori of Camden's Architects Department, assisted by Ken Adie. Hungarian-born, Tábori had studied at Regent Street Polytechnic under Neave Brown and Richard Rogers, and worked variously with Ernö Goldfinger and Denys

Lasdun. The structural engineers were Ove Arup & Partners, while A E Symes Ltd was the main contractor. Symes, a long-established firm, went bankrupt, victims of spiralling inflation. When work stopped, the site fell prey to vandals, and squatters moved in. When a new contractor was appointed, some of the materials used were found to be defective, so that much of the completed work had to be demolished and rebuilt. By the time Stage 1 was completed in 1978, its cost had virtually doubled.

The Estate comprises six parallel terraces, stepping up the hill from the plateau below and neatly filling the sloping site. The 273 dwellings met government density targets without resorting to high-rise, and the 4-storey blocks are so ingeniously arranged that all four floors are rarely visible at one time, with consequent low-rise effect. With its horizontal concrete bands, bold vertical cross-walls, and upper storeys set back, the estate displays similarities with the contemporary Brunswick Centre in Bloomsbury and Neave Brown's Alexandra Road Estate in South Hampstead. A clever use of steps and bridges ensures that each household has its own front door. The development was not originally called the Whittington Estate. It was felt important that tenants should not feel they were on an 'estate', rather living in conventionally numbered houses in a new, named street. Planting was an important feature of the original

scheme, extending the greenery of the neighbouring cemetery towards the east. Trees rise from the 265-space underground car park beneath.

Walk to the end of Lulot Gardens, and turn left down the footway that follows the Estate's western boundary. On your right is the Eastern Cemetery. A proposal by its owners to erect a high 'Berlin Wall', wholly isolating the cemetery from the Estate, was mercifully thwarted.

Passing the end of **RETCAR PLACE**, the next pedestrian street down, reach the Estate's central open space, with a sports pitch to your right. Part way along the linear grassed area on the left is the site of the forked junction where Retcar and Lulot Streets once met. Stop now to consider their odd names. According to *Old Streets of Highgate*, Retcar Street was so called from an anagram of the name of "a whimsical builder called Carter", but this is only partly correct. Ratebooks suggest that the builder of Retcar Street was one Alfred Geard, born in Montacute (Somerset), living in Camberwell and later to move to Archway Road. The first owner of almost all of Lulot Street was Robert Barr, a Battersea builder hailing from Rochester and subsequently a resident of Highgate's North Hill. The pair acquired their respective plots in 1881 from two brothers, Edwin Alfred and Frederick Charles Carter, young Battersea-born "surveyors and auctioneers" living in

Wandsworth. It is their surname that lives on cryptically in Highgate. The name of Frederick's wife was Charlotte; perhaps its second syllable influenced that of 'Lulot'. Edwin Alfred, at 25, was already a widower. Had his late wife given birth to a child, and was the infant Louise Carter who died in Wandsworth, "aged 0", in 1877 his daughter? And did her forename inspire Lulot's first syllable? It is a pleasing, if speculative, notion. Edwin, incidentally, later remarried and changed his career, becoming a Baptist minister, an associate of Spurgeon and eventually President of the Baptist Pioneer Mission. In 1955 some fifty Lulot Street residents petitioned St Pancras Council for the street to be renamed, claiming that the silly-sounding 'Lulot' name was a cause of mirth, and a hindrance to them when they applied for jobs. A proposal that it be renamed 'Gillman Crescent', after James Gillman, local surgeon and friend to Coleridge (p 26), was successively referred to three meetings of St Pancras Council and two of the LCC. It was eventually rejected, objections having been received. The Lulot name was not only retained, but later perpetuated in the naming of modern Lulot Gardens.

Two-storey bay-windowed houses lined both Retcar and Lulot Streets. According to contemporary accounts, the standard of building was extraordinarily low. In 1889 Rev. James Mahomed, curate of St Anne's

Brookfield, wrote of No.26 Lulot Street (home to a sick parishioner) that "the walls are simply wet…the carpet is rotted… the iron bedstead is red with rust. I saw these houses being built. Their erection ought not to have been permitted." A year later, and referring to the New Town generally, the *Hampstead & Highgate Express* complained that "the whole district has obtained an unenviable reputation of being hopelessly insanitary. It is known that many houses have no damp courses or foundations and floor boards are laid straight on the ground." If such reports were accurate, it is amazing that the houses concerned were still occupied 70 years later.

Charles Booth, in December 1898, walked the local streets in order to update his well-known poverty map, with Inspector Mountfield of the Highgate & Upper Holloway sub-division of the Metropolitan Police. He graded Retcar Street a 'fairly comfortable' pink on his poverty scale. Lulot Street he described as "of something of the same style   but with a poorer class of occupants", shading it a 'mixed' purple. Set back from Retcar Street at No.22A were the "tumble-down disreputable-looking buildings of the Highgate [Liberal &] Radical Club". In earlier years the premises had housed a 'Gospel Mission Hall', possibly the forerunner of that in Winscombe Street (p 96). Adjacent, off the east side of Retcar Street lay a triangular yard called Retcar Mews, occupied from

Victorian times by the Norfolk Laundry, whose shop adjoined at No.157 Dartmouth Park Hill. It still traded after WWII as Westcott's Sweet Clean Laundry, by that time sharing the Mews with Livingston Laboratories, makers of electronic measuring instruments.

During WWII both Retcar and Lulot Streets suffered enemy bombing, and some houses at the north end of the latter were recorded as damaged 'beyond repair'. In 1970, not long before it was finally pulled down, Retcar Street was briefly home to the Benburb Centre, an Irish social centre for young people founded in 1970 by Father Collum McDonnell (Benburb, in Dungannon, was the scene of a decisive Irish military victory over the Scots and English in 1646). No.9, the corner shop at the forked junction with Lulot Street, had become a feline boarding-house called 'Cats on Holiday' [24].

Muswell Hillbillies, The Kinks' album of 1971, contains a photo of the pop group posing on the corner, showing houses in both streets behind hoardings and awaiting demolition. The name of the cattery subsequently crossed the Atlantic, adopted as its own by an Ohio rock band influenced by The Kinks.

Now walk on ahead, past the end of the next terrace down, **SANDSTONE PLACE**. Its name presumably alludes to the sand-coloured concrete used in the Estate's construction, much of it painted cream in 1995.

At a T-junction, the footway meets **STONELEIGH TERRACE**, the lowest of the four pedestrian streets. The twin metal chimneys here serve a system providing communal heating to 600-800 households on this and neighbouring estates. Peer over the wall into the cavernous entrance to the underground car park. A high-level walkway here was to have linked up with a 'Stage 2' development to the south that never materialised. Turn back east to return to Dartmouth Park Hill, passing **No.8**, where

on successive London Open House days, visitors have been treated to an enthusiastic talk on the estate, with a guided tour.

Descend the steps to regain **DARTMOUTH PARK HILL**. The terraced houses that lined the west side here, once pretentiously named Park Villas, included among their earliest occupants an umbrella maker and a bird preserver. After WWI, No.167 housed Arthur Jutting, a 'naturalist' or taxidermist.

Turning south, pause at the junction with Raydon Street (see below). Eastward

lies Islington's Girdlestone Estate, fronted by the modern New Brunswick pub, on a site which underwent an interesting transition from Victorian Primitive Methodist Church to fountain-pen factory to watering-hole. Towerless red-brick **St Peter's** church beyond, dating from 1879-80 and designed by C L Luck, is now redundant and converted into apartments. The 'Highgate New Town' name was originally applied equally to streets on the Islington side of the road, dropping down towards Junction Road and Highgate Hill – also built on land that had been owned by Harry Chester. Nowadays the name refers only to the streets on the Camden side which, however, still share with their easterly neighbours an Upper Holloway (N19) postcode. 'South Highgate' was the area's 19th-century postal address.

At the Raydon Street junction, a post office on the north-east corner faced a beershop called the Warwick Arms, on the south-east corner at No.151. South of here, a mix of houses and shops lined the west side of Dartmouth Park Hill. No.125 was successively home to the Whittington Soap Co. and the Clifton Hygienic Laundry. A stableyard known as Upper Mews lay behind Nos.139-141.

Lining the road today are flats of the **Highgate Newtown Estate** ('New Town' is now conventionally spelt as one word). Tábori's 'Stage 1' plans were originally meant to have been continued southward.

24 'Cats on Holiday' on the corner of Lulot Street (left) and Retcar Street (1960s photo: the late John Gay)

Further new terraces were to have covered the large triangular site south of Raydon Street, in a similar style to those of the Whittington Estate. These plans were dropped after the problems with Stage 1. A substitute, 'high tech' Stage 2 scheme never really got off the ground; it was abandoned with only two blocks completed (see pp 93 and 99). By the mid-1970s avant-garde architecture for housing was falling out of favour, lower densities were being prescribed, and council houses with gardens were back in fashion. So Stage 3 here, dating from 1978-81 and designed by Camden Council architects Bill Forrest and Oscar Palacio, comprises more conventional flats and houses, with pitched roofs and built in yellow brick. Although brown brick was originally specified to blend in with the surviving older terraces, yellow was allowed as a compromise.

Turn west along **RAYDON STREET**, which was named in 1866, apparently after a Suffolk village near Ipswich, Harry Chester's birthplace. On the south side is a row of pleasing Stage 3 brick cottages, while the north side is bounded wholly by the south face of Stoneleigh Terrace. The Whittington Estate car-park entrance marks the point where Retcar Street once began its ascent.

Look left along **DOYNTON STREET,** where further modern cottages at **Nos.2-14** are set back at an angle behind a triangular lawn. In the 1970s, houses in Doynton Street and Balmore Street (see below), only recently done up to serve as temporary housing, were invaded by squatters. A Council proposal to demolish them solely to prevent squatting caused a public outcry, and eventually whole terraces that had been earmarked for demolition were saved and renovated. The 3½-storey terrace on the southwest side of Doynton Street at **Nos.7-35** is largely intact.

Before it was first developed in 1865, the whole triangular area southward to Chester Road (p 95) had been leased by Harry Chester to an odd consortium of three gentlemen: Robert Few of Covent Garden; an elderly West Country clergyman, Rev. John Mervin Prower; and William Ford, a solicitor "of Gray's Inn" and a governor of Highgate School, who lived in the 1860s at Brookfield House (p 78), and whose acquaintance with William Butterfield led to the latter's designing of St Mary Brookfield on Dartmouth Park Hill (south of our area). In 1865 the trio conveyed the land to George Yates, a Sheffield-born builder and "employer of 30 men". Though confirmed only in 1866, the proposed street names were already identified in the deed. Rev. J M Prower, the joint landowner, was both vicar of Purton (Wiltshire), and a canon of Bristol Cathedral. Perhaps coincidentally, the Gloucestershire village of Doynton lay just off the direct route between the two. Early Doynton Street residents included labourers and clerks, a coachsmith, commercial traveller, retired corndealer, and an "organist & professor of music", with a sprinkling of piano makers and railwaymen – and the builder George Yates. No absentee landlord, he moved with his family into now demolished No.1. The standard of building, as Charles Booth remarked in 1898, was "still bad...but better than Colva Street (p 94); letting here chiefly by floors, there by rooms rather: costers etc; untidy women about. Light blue." No.17 was home at the time to Mrs Jane Jarvis, an ostrich feather cleaner.

Continue along **RAYDON STREET**. Among the demolished houses and shops was a pre-WWII beershop at No.27 on the left, while premises known as Doynton Buildings adjoined at No.31. No.37, grandiosely named the North London Dental Surgery in the 1890s, ended its life as a bric-a-brac shop called British Tat. Early tenants at No.39 were three organ builders and their families, a total of 13 people. The 3-storey houses on the north side, now replaced by Stoneleigh Terrace, were described by Booth as "better working class"; Francis Honour was the 19th-century landlord of many of the properties.

Three Point Park was one of 60 names suggested by local people for the newly refurbished play area on the left. Previously closed because of vandalism, it was renovated and reopened in 2006, adorned with mosaics and four enormous,

25 St Anne's temporary mission church & school
(from *St Mary Brookfield Centenary 1875-1975*)

A ... Class room
B ... Church & School room
C ... Carpenter's Shop
D ... Porch
E ... Coal Dust heap

3-dimensional, colourfully painted snakes. The triangular playground marks the corner site of the St Anne's Mission Hall or Church, which served as such until after WWII. In Highgate New Town's earliest days, its "shabby ill-kempt children … started to attend services at St Anne's [Brookfield]. [They] were accommodated on special benches in front of the congregation but as there were immediately complaints to the churchwardens about the smell and fleas, the children were turned out!" A temporary mission church opened [25] on 29 Nov 1868 above a carpenter's workshop on the children's home ground. Its permanent successor in Raydon Street combined spiritual succour with educational and social activity. Successively recorded as the Brookfield Institute (by 1884), as the Brookfield Club & Reading Room (by 1905) and as the St Anne's Men's Social Club after WWI, it became a Church Army Social Centre after WWII.

Just beyond the next turning (Balmore Street), at long-demolished No.43, was the St Pancras Infant Welfare & Artificial Sunlight Centre. The first of its kind in London, it was opened by the Mayor in 1925. Here young "anaemic and debilitated children and sufferers from rickets" were brought to undergo "bottled sunshine treatment". Under-fives, stripped of their clothes and wearing coloured spectacles to protect their sight, were exposed to ultra-violet radiation, at first for no more than a cautious five minutes, although the period was gradually lengthened. Three mornings a week, the treatment was supervised by Dr Beaumont, the honorary medical superintendent. The clinic flourished here until WWII, when the premises were put to industrial use, as the adhesive works of Channon's Patent Glue Co.

Turn sharp left by the playground into **BALMORE STREET**. Opposite stands one of the two blocks completed in the abortive 'Stage 2' pilot redevelopment. Forrest and Palacio's 'high tech', prefabricated 3-storey block of bedsits was completed in 1978. Just two years later the *Architects' Journal* was complaining that the terrace had already weathered badly: it "looked fine when finished – and for a few months after….It now looks like a pair of abandoned trams or the beat-up housing compounds of migrant workers in Africa, and it is hard to believe that it is only three years old." A quarter-century later, the impression is much the same.

Most of the street's terraced houses were saved, to enjoy rehabilitation after the Council's bulldozing mania ended in 1976. **Nos.10-40** on the north side face **Nos.1-39** on the other, all in partially stuccoed yellow stock brick, with bay windows, and front doors at semi-basement level. Walk to the far end of the street. Here in 1972, and while under threat of demolition, No.3 was taken over by members of the Simon Community to house homeless families. In the same year, No.1 became the headquarters of the Friends of the Western Buddhist Order, founded four years earlier to promote Buddhism in Britain. Sangharakshita, its founder, born Dennis Lingwood in South London in 1925, had realised he was a Buddhist at the age of 16. World War II took him to India, where he stayed on to become a monk.

Easily missed on the left is the aptly named **Secret Garden**, a charming oasis created on the site of demolished Nos.2-8 and maintained by the Secret Garden Gang, a hard-working band of local volunteers.

Looking back along the well-treed street, it is hard to believe that this was once considered a slum. It began as Colva Street, named maybe after Colfa (or Colva), a tiny village in Radnorshire (Mervin, Prower's middle name, is suggestive of Welsh extraction); or perhaps after a beach in Portuguese Goa occupied by the British Army during the Napoleonic wars. Although named in 1866, the street was late infill. Fifteen years later only two houses were occupied, and owned, like most of those eventually built on the north side, by Samuel Hensby (cf. Model Dwellings, p 89). Houses opposite, owned by one William B Mason, had been built but were still awaiting tenants.

Premises here at the east end of the street were licensed for religious worship in 1883-86. Walter Harman of Highgate Road (Baptist) Chapel financed and supervised a mission in this "place of considerable spiritual destitution". Average Sunday School attendance was 64, while 30 locals were reported to have "renounced strong drink".

Charles Booth, in 1898, describes Colva Street's 2½-storey houses as "very badly built, 4 or 5 families to a house. The street is not badly built up at the back, but in every other respect one of the worst possible specimens of semi-suburban 'cottage' jerry building. People from Somers Town originally, and character of street and n[eighbour]hood very slightly altered since the first people came in; very little criminal work, but rough and drunken; every appearance of neglect both by owners and occupiers; several untidy ragged children about; one bare-footed boy, the second seen in the whole [district]." Booth coded the street a 'very poor' dark blue. *The Times* in August 1898 reported the prosecution of a group of young thieves based in Colva Street, calling themselves the Dick Turpin gang.

Colva Street was renamed Balmore Street in 1907 after a petition by landlords, who complained that its reputation prevented them from letting to a better class of artisan. The seemingly arbitrary new name, that of a several villages in Scotland, may have been adopted in place of the then overworked 'Balmoral'.

Poverty persisted, however. Sidney Day's reminiscences, published in 2006 as *London Born*, give a vivid account of his 1920s childhood here. The inhabitants took what pride they could in their homes. Doorsteps were regularly whitewashed. Their residents would often sit outside when conditions indoors became intolerable; "millions of bugs" bred behind the lime-washed matchboard that substituted for wallpaper. Sidney's childhood was an outdoor one; he was forever doing odd jobs. From the age of six he collected horse dung from the streets, which was then hawked from door to door at one penny (or more) a bucketful. Pastimes included bird-nesting, egg collecting and the netting of wild birds in the grounds of Kenwood or Holly Lodge, to serve either as food or as caged songbirds (of which Day's father kept a dozen). Also popular was juvenile street-fighting, in which the "Tiger Bay Mob" confronted the "Raydon and Doighton [sic] Street Mobs". Balmore Street was commonly known as 'Tiger Bay'. This nickname was coined by 19th-century sailors for certain dockland areas where, through theft or assault, they suffered 'ferocious' ill-treatment at the hands of the inhabitants; the 'she-tigers' (prostitutes) were reputedly the worst. Most famously assigned to the area that is now called Cardiff Bay, the sobriquet was also applied to several notorious streets in London's East End, as well as being somehow brought to landlocked Colva Street – by servicemen returning from India, according to Sidney Day. By whatever route the nickname arrived here, local men in pub brawls certainly "fought like tigers".

Once adjoining No.1 were three assorted buildings: No.1A, occupied in Victorian times by a firm of druggists' sundries manufacturers, and for much of the 20th century by the Brookfield Social Club; No.1B, once named Colva Cottage; and No.1C, workshops of the monumental masons living at adjacent No.18 Chester Road (p 96). Here today is the entrance to **COLVA WALK**; pause here to view a short row of homely modern 2-storey brick cottages to the right, while curving away to the left is a handsome 3-storey terrace

with overhanging eaves, timber trellises and small, brightly painted balconies – a delightful product of Forrest and Palacio's Stage 3 work. The project was much praised, winning a Civic Trust Award in 1983, while Tábori's more daring Stage 1 scheme was largely ignored.

Once running north and south off the east end of Balmore Street were two narrow cul-de-sacs, together known as Colva Mews. Here a blacksmith still plied his trade in 1912; and here was stabled the donkey that pulled a firewood dealer's cart, and which (as Sidney Day recalls) bled to death after slipping on an icy Dartmouth Park Hill. Its loss was remedied by "lifting" a horse from Express Dairies, who grazed their animals on the Kenwood estate.

Both Balmore and Doynton Streets once continued east, debouching into Dartmouth Park Hill. Now isolated from the latter, the two streets are linked by a modern roadway on the line of Colva Mews North, together forming a loop. Covered walkways allow pedestrian access from each street to the main road. Walk through the one straight ahead, noting the decoration overhead, compared by one observer to that of a Maori longhouse.

Emerging into **DARTMOUTH PARK HILL**, look to the left. Curving along the west side are the Stage 3 apartments, 3-storey to match the surviving terraces opposite, brick-built with pitched roofs, and divided by projecting staircases into

pairs of 'villas'. Originally named Brookfield Terrace, this stretch of road was lined (as Charles Booth recorded) by "mainly 2/3-st[orey] houses, some shops, working-class and not of the best kind"; "pink, low-grade" was his verdict. On the former Doynton Street corner stood the Brookfield public house. As was often the case in new working-class areas, this was among the first buildings to be erected in Highgate New Town. Sidney Day further recalls that in the 1920s, on Sunday mornings, customers brought their favourite birds to the pub in carrying-cages, which they placed on a shelf running the length of the bar. Bets were then placed on the birds' singing ability, and competitions held to decide which had the best plumage.

Turn right, and walk south to the junction with Chester Road. Southward lies Dartmouth Park, the middle-class Victorian neighbourhood developed on land owned by the Earl of Dartmouth, and from which Dartmouth Park Hill took its name, when the upper reaches of Maiden Lane (p 85) were renamed in 1873.

Turning right again, into **CHESTER ROAD**, cross over to enjoy a fine view of the distant spire of St Michael's Church (p 27) set atop a thickly wooded hillside. The road was named after landowner Harry Chester of South Grove House (p 27), the husband of Anna Maria Chester, granddaughter of Thomas Bromwich, the 18th-century owner of Chester's house.

Very active in Highgate village life, Chester was President of the HLSI. A senior civil servant, he was Secretary to the Privy Council Committee on Education, and as a keen promoter of popular education was a prime mover in the establishment of Highgate's National & Industrial Schools. It is ironic that the estate of such a man should have developed into a near-slum. Chester Road, however, was one of the area's more respectable streets, mostly shaded a 'fairly comfortable' pink on Booth's poverty map. The gabled red-brick villas on the left at **Nos.1-19**, then recently built, even rated a 'middle class' red. Note the terracotta tiling on their gables.

To your right is **No.2**, a straggling white-painted concrete building was built as a Camden Council mental health hostel in 1972-76, and still serves that purpose. (A Family Health Centre for the neighbourhood was to have been erected nearby, but the proposal was eventually dropped for lack of support from local doctors.) On the site previously were a short terrace (Nos.1-4 Cornwall Villas), a pair of semi-detached houses called Chester Villas, and a larger Plevna Villa (named after a Bulgarian town famously besieged by the Turks until relieved by the Russians in 1877). This house's first occupants were Thomas and Henry Durnford, local builders who may have lent their name to Durnford Terrace (now Marsden Street) in West Kentish Town.

West of here some original houses survive, a few renovated by Camden Council c.1976. On the north side at **Nos.18-56**, the long 3-storey range with front gardens was at first known as Chester Terrace. No.18 (once Ebenezer House) was successively home to two monumental masons, Thomas Lamerton in the 19th century and Frederick Sainsbury in the next. Both used workshops behind at No.1C Colva (Balmore) Street. Monumental masonry was a considerable local industry, obviously attracted here by the nearby cemetery. No.18 was also (in 1899) the address of the North London United Gospel Temperance Committee.

Land opposite, described as 'Lot 5' – a two-acre field that had been leased in 1804 by John Oliver of the Bull & Last – was conveyed in 1863 by Harry Chester, with Messrs Few, Ford and Prower (see p 92), to one Percival Smith, a manufacturing chemist of Bow Common. It was quickly leased on to James Curtis, a Euston Road zinc worker, and here were laid out two cul-de-sacs, lined by some of the area's earliest-built houses. **WINSCOMBE STREET** was named in 1865, seemingly after the Somerset village, quite why is unclear. By 1872, a John Watson owned most of the houses; there was already overcrowding, and two houses were home to over 20 people. Charles Booth later coded the street a 'mixed' purple. Walk down the street, between **Nos.1-15** on the left, 3½-storey

with steep steps up to each front door, and **Nos.2-14** opposite, 3-storey with no basement area.

At the bottom, in late-Victorian times, was a tennis court, for the use of well-heeled residents of nearby Dartmouth Park. Here today is a modern north-facing terrace of five houses (plus a studio), designed by Neave Brown and constructed in concrete and flint-lime brick. They were erected in 1963-64 by a housing association formed for the purpose, with Brown as a member. The houses are 2½-storey at the front and 3 at the rear, taking advantage of the sloping site. Each front door is reached by a short spiral staircase in a concrete drum. The interiors were 'zoned', with the top floor intended for adult use, the middle storey as the family area, and the lower floor for children. The first residents, all professionals, included the engineer Anthony Hunt, who worked on the Eden Project in Cornwall. One of the first residents, at **No.26,** was the architect Edward Jones, more recently the co-designer, with Sir Jeremy Dixon, of the new Opera House for Covent Garden and the Ondaatje Wing at the National Portrait Gallery; meanwhile, living at **No.32** were Michael and Patti Hopkins, later designers of the Glyndebourne Opera House and the MPs' offices at Westminster known as Portcullis House.

In the street's southwest corner stands the former non-denominational People's Gospel Mission Hall, still thus boldly inscribed. It is dated 1892 and on the south face are four inscribed stones for J C Randall, Richard Avery, a friend, and M J Lynn. 100 people attended the Sunday morning service here in Edwardian times; older locals fondly remember the magic-lantern shows they enjoyed as children. Still known in the 1970s as the Winscombe Mission, the building was later called the Winscombe Hall, until taken over as part of the Highgate Newtown Youth Club; today it forms part of the Fresh Youth Academy (p 98).

Return to **CHESTER ROAD** and turn left, past Nos.41-45, noting the original railings with fleur-de-lys finials. Frederick Deacon, another monumental mason, lived before WWII at **No.41**. From 1868 the same house (at that time No.9) was home to Chelsea-born Alfred Joseph Woolmer (1806-92), a prolific literary and historical genre painter, and a member of the Society of British Artists. In his sixty-year career, over 400 of his works were exhibited in London, twelve of them at the Royal Academy. Woolmer was noted for his nostalgically romantic illustrations in the published editions of major poets; and according to the *DNB*, was "best known for sensuous, mildly erotic images of ladies at their *toilette* and for elegant courtship scenes set in light-dappled gardens and shady bowers". Woolmer's private life is obscure. Although he is recorded here as "married", his wife Mary Anne, who lived with him

at his previous home in Fortis Green, is intriguingly absent from later census returns. Alfred lived in Chester Road with his widowed elder sister and his daughter Marion, herself an accomplished exhibiting artist, before moving to Dartmouth Park Avenue in 1875.

The public house on the next corner, which was latterly called the Holly Lodge, after the long-demolished home of Baroness Burdett-Coutts (p 101), has recently become a gastropub named **The Star**. For over a century it was called the Totnes Castle. The Devonshire town was the birthplace of Richard Harris, the builder responsible for many of the adjacent houses.

Turn left again, down the second of the two cul-de-sacs, still-cobbled **BERTRAM STREET**, so named in 1865 for reasons unknown. Two almost identical 3-storey terraces face each other, part-stuccoed, with large rectangular windows, diminutive front yards and modern railings. Notice on the left, at **No.10**, the inscription set in the narrow rectangular fanlight and proclaiming the house's unusually honest name – Brickview! Despite the antique lettering, this was probably a late addition; other similar lights in the street are of plain glass. Most early residents of the street worked in the building trade, as bricklayers, carpenters, plasterers, painters or plumbers. Many had families, and 22 people were living at No.1 in 1871. House ownership was by then

already divided between several different landlords, including Samuel Lamble, the Kentish Town builder and St Pancras vestryman; and members of the Eungblut family, piano makers of Camden Town. Colouring the street a 'mixed' purple, Charles Booth remarked in 1898 that "broken windows [were] not uncommon".

Two years later, the local enthusiasm for bird netting (see p 94) was confirmed by a report in *The Times*. Jim Pettifer, a young brass finisher of Bertram Street, was caught red-handed in woods on Lord Mansfield's Kenwood estate and charged with the taking of six wild birds – two chaffinches, a blackbird, thrush, blackcap and nuthatch. The Hampstead Bench fined him 5 shillings (25p) per bird, and 10s for wilful damage to a fence, or in default 7 days' imprisonment with hard labour.

At the end of the street a gateway leads into the **Highgate Newtown Community Centre**. The first buildings on this site were the St Anne's (Brookfield) National Schools, built here in the early 1870s on land donated by Baroness Burdett-Coutts, and to a Gothic design by church architect John Pollard Seddon of Grove Terrace. There were, strictly, three separate schools – for boys, girls and infants – and each section had its own house for the mistress or master. Former pupils remember parents paying one penny ($\frac{1}{2}$p) a week for their education. Each afternoon the infants were made to lie down on canvas beds, and rewarded with two 'dolly mixture' sweets if they slept. The school closed in 1947, to be replaced by a Territorial Army Centre. On your left stand three garages that were used to house tanks. The buildings were later used as training workshops for prisoners from Pentonville Prison. Then in 1981 it was taken over by the community, and with the help of voluntary organisations and a committee of local people it has become a thriving centre of local life, whose wide-ranging activities extend from astronomy and telescope making to Persian aerobic dance. A youth club was established in 1987, with Camden Council and ILEA support, using the old tank garages and Winscombe Hall (p 97). They now house the Fresh Youth Academy, offering accredited courses in drama, dance, sport, IT and video film-making. On the other side of the site another tank garage is now used as the family centre. Do look round if you are here when the Community Centre is open (Mondays-Fridays); there is a café for light refreshments.

Returning to Bertram Street, pass through a gap in the wall on the left. It leads to a footpath, on reaching which turn right. This is the last vestige of an ancient right of way that ran northeast across the fields from the Bull & Last pub in Highgate Road to Maiden Lane (Dartmouth Park Hill). The path's two ends were extinguished long ago, and this middle section has lost much of its original

purpose. Regaining Chester Road, notice how the footway continues briefly on the other side, to Balmore Street. Beyond there, former Retcar Street was built on the line of the path.

On your right is **No.53 Chester Road**, which as No.21 was the 19th-century home of a further monumental mason, George Prickett Mills. Land west of here formed part of Oak Tree Field, 10 acres leased for grazing in 1804 by Charles Lane, a butcher of Angel Row (p 31). It remained largely undeveloped until the 20th century. **Nos.55&57** are two blocks of 'Homes for Heroes' built in the 1920s here on the northern edge of the Brookfield Estate (p 112).

Trespassing briefly into Route 6, turn into **CROFTDOWN ROAD** (p 112), walk partway down and cross over to admire the new rear **gates** of Brookfield Primary School (p 100). Featuring a colourful collage of artwork created entirely by the schoolchildren, they were constructed by Chris Plowman, a sculptural artist, following the pupils' designs.

Backtrack past a doorway inscribed "The Children's Corner". This was the entrance to the former junior section of **Highgate Library**. Added at the back of the main building, top-lit and with oak fittings scaled down to child size, it opened in 1936. To mark the occasion [26] the children received a special message from the poet Walter de la Mare. The Children's Corner closed in the 1970s, deemed too

expensive to staff separately, and the space is now the base of the Mobile Library and the Home Library Service to the housebound.

Return to **CHESTER ROAD** and turn left to view the main part of the library, which celebrated its centenary in 2006. This was the first public library in St Pancras, and for decades the only one to be purpose-built, other branches being opened in converted houses or shops. The Vestry was a reluctant and belated adopter of the Public Library Act (1850); ratepayers, in successive referendums, were resistant to the cost. Progress was made after the formation of the new borough council in 1900: referendums were no longer a requirement and the Progressive (Liberal) party gained control. Andrew Dale Carnegie, the Scottish-born American steel magnate, donated £4,000 to St Pancras to pay for a central library in Kentish Town (which never materialised) and for four branch libraries. The Council was to raise a penny rate to cover running expenses and to provide the land. The chosen site in Chester Road, scarcely the most central or accessible in the borough, was sold cheaply by Mr Burdett-Coutts (né Bartlett, p 104), the Duke of Bedford meeting its £500 cost. Designed in a Renaissance style by William Nisbet-Blair, the borough engineer, the mostly red-brick building has a pedimented central section with an arched loggia, flanked by lower wings. The foundation stone was laid on 14 June 1906 by Cllr H T Ashby, and the library was enthusiastically opened just four months later, on 18 October, by George Hickling, the Mayor.

In the early days there was no browsing of the shelves; books were on closed access, readers selecting them from a catalogue 'indicator'. Despite its awkward location, the Highgate branch served as the headquarters of the St Pancras library service. Here all books were catalogued, a junior assistant then carrying them to other branches in a suitcase, by tram from Parliament Hill Fields. Between 1947 and 1965 the library organised a wide range of extension activities, including poetry and gramophone circles, and numerous talks and debates. Speakers included Neville Cardus, Huw Weldon, Noel Streatfeild, Stella Gibbons, Enid Blyton, Valentine Dyall and Eleanor Bron. A regular visitor in the 1960s was the historian A J P Taylor. Under the area's Stage 2 redevelopment plans, the library was meant to be demolished and replaced, but was saved largely through community action. In 1980, with Camden Lottery funding, the interior was nicely remodelled by John Winter & Associates, with Peter McMunn as project architect, but their thoughtful work had, sadly, been undone by the end of the decade. The building was Grade-II Listed in 1995. Outside, behind original railings, is a garden with a seat, created in 2004 in memory of Edith Morgan, late Secretary of the Friends of Highgate Library (FOHL), a very active user group supported by such celebrities as writer/broadcaster Hunter Davies and actor Roger Lloyd Pack.

Opposite is one end of the local shopping parade (1976-78), another of the two blocks completed under Forrest and Palacio's pilot Stage 2 plans. The 'high-tech' 4-storey block at **Nos.58-86** is in reinforced concrete, with bolted coloured enamelled concrete panels and painted railings. Shops occupy the two lower levels, with maisonettes above. The parade's construction was a high priority,

26 The Children's Corner, Highgate Library: opening ceremony, 9 Oct 1936 (*Sunday Pictorial*), with children waiting to be presented with something, perhaps a copy of Walter de la Mare's message

as the shops it was meant to replace had already been demolished. No.82 today houses the Fresh Juice bar and gymnasium, run in conjunction with the Fresh Youth Academy. No.60 is the base of the Highgate Newtown Neighbourhood Partnership (HNNP), a fund-raising and co-ordinating body for local initiatives. The same address was home in 1892 to the Highgate Radical & Liberal Club, later removed to Retcar Street.

Set on a small grassy mound, at the acute-angled junction with Raydon Street, is a sculpture called *Diversity*. Two giant metal hands, one brown and one white, flank a human figure in the form of a chair, with a face half white and half brown. As a plaque declares, it was designed by Carlee Hooker and Katy Donovan, sculpted by Kevin Harrison, and funded by Groundwork Camden and the 1995 Camden Greening Forum Award – in memory of "Anthony Antoniou, a friend to all who is greatly missed by his community, a tragic loss of a talented young man". Anthony, a local boy, had died in a traffic accident.

Standing on this corner in the 1880s was the Chester Coffee Tavern at No.72. Adjoining were the workshops of monumental masons Millward & Co.; they were shown as a bombed "ruin" on a post-WWII map, though the firm remained in business here into the 1960s. Cross to the end of Stoneleigh Terrace, where at former No.74 Chester Road fellow stonemasons Henry Daniel & Co. likewise continued trading; as did yet another chiseler, George Richard Langley of nearby No.66 Raydon Street.

Now follow Chester Road as it swings southward. Lined on one side by the leafy Eastern Cemetery, it soon feels more suburban. On your right are the locked gates of the cemetery's disused, once important, south entrance. To its right stood the Cemetery Lodge, whose black shading on the WWII bomb-damage map suggests "total destruction". Post-war graves now occupy its site.

Opposite stand the red-brick flats of **Chester House**, an outpost of the Brookfield Estate (p 112), built in a similar style to the Croftdown Road blocks and of similar 1920s vintage.

Next on the left is **Brookfield Primary School**, first opened in 1914 as an LCC elementary school. From 1931 it housed the Burghley Central School for Girls, relocated from Burghley Road in Kentish Town. Ahead of the school building, notice on a gatepost the fading painted legend "RB No.1": At the time of the Blitz, Burghley Central served as a Reinforcement Base of the Auxiliary Fire Service (AFS). Here firefighters from outside London were assembled before assignment to parts of the capital under stress. The girls' school's domestic science equipment was a factor in its selection as a Reinforcement Base: hot meals could be cooked for hungry firemen. Also based here for a while were some of the many London taxis requisitioned by the AFS to tow trailer pumps. The cabs proved to be underpowered for the job and most were returned to the ranks, although some drivers remained in the AFS, serving with distinction. Renamed Brookfield County Secondary School for Girls after WWII, the building was remodelled in 1965-66 as a primary school; the top hall and new classrooms were added. Burghley Junior boys and girls then moved north from Kentish Town, later to be joined by the Burghley Infants. With the formal merger of the schools in 1981, today's Brookfield Primary came into being. Continue past its Chester Road entrance, where the arch above, like the gates in Croftdown Road (p 98), was executed by Chris Plowman using the children's designs.

Beyond **No.63**, presumably the caretaker's house, is a neo-Georgian block at **Nos.65-69** comprising three flats. **Nos.71&73**, a pair of semi-detached villas once respectively named Shirley and Somerville, were for some years the only buildings in this part of Chester Road; No.71 sports an incongruous suburban-style bow window.

Finally, at No.75, we pass the **Konstam Children's Centre**, a Council-run facility offering nursery education and childcare. First opened on 17 March

1923 as the Highgate New Town Clinic, it later became a Wartime Day Nursery, and then an LCC Day Nursery, before under Camden control it assumed its present name. This recalls Mr & Mrs Kohnstamm (*sic*) of Hampstead, who established the original clinic in memory of their two sons, who lost their lives in WWI.

Summing up his impressions of Highgate New Town in 1898, Charles Booth described it as "a small area that stands in no very good repute. There is no particular explanation save that the first people who came gave it a rather bad name and public opinion has been by way of hanging it ever since". Today it houses a mixed, multicultural population, families that have lived locally for four generations joined by others with roots in every part of the globe. While not immune to the social problems of any inner-city area, the New Town retains a strong community spirit fostered by three residents' associations, the community centre, the FOHL and the HNNP.

Rounding a second bend in the road, and passing on the left picturesque Holly Village (p 110), reach Swain's Lane and turn left. Take the local bus from here towards Archway or Swiss Cottage, or continue ahead to the end of the Lane and the Parliament Hill Fields terminus, where the next Route can be joined.

Route 6
Holly Lodge and the Coutts estate
Downhill walk from Holly Lodge Gardens to Swain's Lane
For modern map see back cover

On this walk we explore an outlying estate, first settled by the Coutts family in the early 19th century, and centred on their mansion, Holly Lodge. This was the summer retreat of the fabulously wealthy Angela, Baroness Burdett-Coutts. She died in 1906, and when the house with its gardens and model farm was finally sold in 1923 the Holly Lodge Estate was constructed. Its garden suburb atmosphere survives to this day. The rest of the estate land, bought as a protection against the rapid advance of housing and new cemeteries in the middle of the 19th century, became covered with new houses of a slightly different kind.

Buses are the only form of public transport in this part of north London. The walk begins by the entrance to Holly Lodge Gardens on **HIGHGATE WEST HILL.** Alight at the 'Holly Lodge' bus stop if you are approaching from Highgate village, or at the 'Merton Lane' bus stop if you are coming from the south. Here we describe what can be seen from the bus as it climbs West Hill, following the western boundary of the Holly Lodge Estate. Those who

have alighted at the Parliament Hill Fields terminus may decide to walk up the hill.

First, note St Anne's church (p 83), for which the Baroness provided a peal of bells. Next follows **Nos.91-105**, a row of 1920s detached Holly Lodge Estate houses, which unlike most other houses on the Estate front a public road. The site of the first house (No.105, home in the late 1960s to Camden's first woman mayor, Millie Miller) was marked as the main entrance to the Coutts' grounds on the 1915 OS map; the 1922 sale map shows a "New Carriageway" leading northwards from it. The bus then passes the most southerly of the Holly Lodge Estate roads, Langbourne Avenue. There is no entrance for motor vehicles here, nor at the following two turnings, Makepeace and Oakeshott Avenues. The latter marks the approximate position of the Coutts' model farm, and beyond is the site of its dairy. North of this was the lodge to the main 19th-century carriage entrance, still marked by Egyptian style gateposts, surviving at the start of a rather hidden turning called Robin Grove. Ring the bell now for the 'Merton Lane' stop. Cross carefully over Highgate West Hill and walk back down the other side, passing the stepped entrance to Holly Terrace (see p 72) which was also part of the Coutts' estate. Beyond, note two bollards on the pavement which remain from a (covered) side entrance to former Holly Lodge that we describe below.

The walk proper begins at the entrance to **HOLLY LODGE GARDENS** from Highgate West Hill. You cannot miss the various notices warning that it is a private estate, but pedestrians are allowed to walk through. Only residents are eligible for a parking permit, so motorists must park elsewhere. Pass through the gate and pause on the right, by railings overlooking the lawn.

From 1741 the site of Holly Terrace, just to the north, and 13 acres east of Highgate West Hill were owned by the Cooke family. They employed George Smart to develop the northern part of their lands. He began Holly Terrace in 1807 and, at about the same time, the house that came to be known as Holly Lodge, on the site of the present **Nos.2&3** on our left. The house was originally known as Hollybush Lodge. Holly is quite common locally on Hampstead Heath, but many holly trees were also planted on the estate.

Sir Henry Tempest leased the house in 1808 and in the following year sub-let it to a young actress called Harriot Mellon. She was the mistress of Thomas Coutts, an elderly, extremely rich banker. After his wife died in 1815, he married Harriot and used his wealth to improve and enlarge the estate. That same year he bought adjacent land south of where Oakeshott Avenue now lies, with Swain's Lane as its southern and eastern boundaries.

It was a happy marriage, and when Thomas Coutts died in 1822 he left Harriot the whole of his fortune. Society regarded her as an adventuress who had preyed on an old man; she was caricatured and mocked for her extravagant lifestyle and her generous giving to the poor. In 1827, aged 49, she married the 26-year-old William Aubrey de Vere, 9th Duke of St Albans. This union was also successful, but was regarded as an exchange of wealth for a title, and Harriot was never admitted into aristocratic circles.

Harriot had the grounds landscaped in 1825 by John Buonarotti Papworth. Most of this pleasant landscaping has disappeared, but a small area of the original tree planting now stands in mature splendour to our right. The 1907 house-sale brochure mentioned these trees, "over the tops of which the electric light of the House of Commons, four miles distant, is seen at night". As the estate developed, "an impenetrable screen of foliage" was planted "all round that portion of the property which is bounded by public roads…giving to the whole the impression of a country estate rather than one lying within a great city".

Harriot, who had become a partner in Coutts' bank and proved to be an excellent businesswoman, apparently thought carefully about who should inherit her fortune. When she died in 1837, she left the house and nearly all her money to her first husband's granddaughter, Angela Burdett (1814-1906), daughter of the radical politician Sir Francis Burdett (who had actually advised Coutts, his father-in-law, against marriage to Harriot). Angela became the richest woman in England after Queen Victoria. Harriot's will stipulated that her successors take the surname of Coutts; Angela Burdett did so, appending it to her own, though she was often known simply as Miss Coutts. It was not until after the death of the Duke of St Albans in 1849 that Holly Lodge reverted to her and she came to use it as her summer country retreat. She had already inherited a very grand house in Stratton Street, Mayfair and had also bought a seaside property in Torquay.

The constant social activities (e.g. **[27]**) at the 'big house' from 1849 until her death in 1906 must have been of great interest to the local populace. (Highgate was not short of the rich and illustrious at this time, and attracted other circles of influential people.) The local parish magazine in 1871 listed the numbers of visitors to Holly Lodge that year. Queen Victoria and the royal family were frequent guests. The Archbishop of Canterbury was on the list, as were foreign royalty and heads of state; so too were people interested in the arts and social reform. Poorer people came in large

27 'Reception of the Belgian Volunteers by Miss Burdett Coutts, at Holly Lodge' (*Illustrated London News*, 27 July 1867)

numbers on outings by horse and wagon. The Baroness had known Charles Dickens well before she inherited the estate, and he came here often. He buried his young daughter Dora in open ground in the new cemetery above her house; her gardener helped to prepare the grave. She relied on his help with her early charity work, but was quite unable to countenance his legal separation from his wife in 1858. Without his support, Urania Cottage, the home for prostitutes she had opened in Shepherd's Bush, failed, and although they continued to correspond, the close friendship was over.

For, like most of her contemporaries in high society, Miss Coutts lived her life by a narrow set of rules of conduct. It is therefore all the more surprising that in 1881, at the age of 67, she defied convention and married a man 37 years her junior, and a foreigner. Her new husband was her American assistant, William Lehman Ashmead Bartlett, the son of one of her neighbours in Torquay. He took her surname. Under the terms of Harriot's will, Angela's inheritance was conditional on the heiress not marrying an alien. The Queen was alarmed by the union and there was shock and consternation among her friends and family. Her sister took legal action and as a result the Baroness's fortune was reduced by 60 per cent. Yet it is generally considered by her biographers that the marriage was a happy one. It is possible that she turned to Bartlett for support after she had lost the friendship and help of her beloved companion Mrs Hannah Brown, who had died in 1878. Since Angela's youth, Hannah had remained at her side and Hannah's husband, Dr William Brown, also became a loyal and trustworthy supporter.

On account of her largesse over the years to a great variety of charitable causes, and at Gladstone's suggestion, Angela was in 1871 created a Baroness [28]. She chose to be called Baroness Burdett-Coutts of Brookfield and Highgate; Brookfield was the land at the south end of West Hill (p 78). A year later she was presented with the Freedom of the City of London, the first woman thus honoured, and a year later with that of Edinburgh. After her death in 1906 she was buried in Westminster Abbey.

Her husband then put the property on the market. However, it was not until after his death in 1921 that it began to sell. The main house and 55 acres of land, now known as the Holly Lodge Estate, were sold in 1923 to Abraham Davis for £45,000 (£205,000 had been the asking price in 1907). Davis was a St Pancras councillor who took a leading part in post-1919 public housing construction in the borough and in other parts of London, promoting soundly built blocks of flats and exploiting subsidised government housing finance. He often acted as his own architect. Here, he wanted to build a wholly middle-class

28 The millionaire philanthropist Baroness Burdett-Coutts: cartoon entitled 'Money' (*The Hornet*, 31 July 1872)

garden suburb. Plans were drawn up and work started, but after Abraham's death, on 28 January 1924, alterations to the layout in response to unexpectedly heavy expenditure on infrastructure resulted in a segment of the eastern estate being designated for blocks of flats for 'lady workers' (see later, p 107).

Holly Lodge itself had been built along the east-west contour of the hill. The yellow drawing-room, conservatory and Long Verandah (the main entertainment salon), all faced south, with splendid views over London and protected from the weather by "the Chestnut Terrace". To the east of the house were the stables. The present entrance to Holly Lodge Gardens did not then exist. At the end of a long sinuous carriageway, a large turning-circle (more or less where we are standing) allowed coaches to deposit visitors at the front steps to the house.

Now walk ahead, following, as far as parked cars will permit, the border of the delightful mature garden on the right. This is all that is left of the original garden and, unfortunately for us, is strictly private. There was once a rose garden "replete with rare specimens". Beyond and to the right was the Ivy Temple, sheltering an old statue of Dick Whittington (West Hill was one of the spots where, according to tradition, he had halted and listened to the sound of Bow Bells in the distance (cf. p 88)). The garden contained cedars of Lebanon and

other alien conifers; the wood from one 193-year-old cedar tree, recently cut down, has been turned into chairs and sculpture by the artist Friedel Buecking, who was inspired by photographs of the gardens of Holly Lodge. These can be seen at the foot of the slope.

Continue walking. The lawn once adjoined Crab Tree Hollow, so named from a single large shrub but which was also planted with individual specimens of different kinds of trees. At the end of the garden look down muddy **ROBIN GROVE**, a gated, unmetalled road, once part of the main carriageway to the house. It leads to eight (originally nine) houses of different sizes, lying hidden among the trees.

Robin Grove was so named in 1924, presumably after the red-breasted bird and as a reminder of its rural past. The houses were among the earliest to be built on the Estate: by 1928 the Central Building Company was advertising houses here for sale at £3,250 to £6,000. No.5 in those early days was the home of Arthur Lowndes Yates MC MD FRCS, co-author of *Principles and Practices of Otology*, and his wife Mary. At No.4 an "experienced chauffeuse" advertised in *The Times* of 23 September 1931, offering a clean licence, running repairs and a reference. Later in the century Conrad Black, the newspaper tycoon, lived with his first wife at No.9. He demolished No.7 to make himself an oversized garden.

The road leads out onto Highgate West Hill. There is no apparent sign of the old lodge that once stood on the south side of the road, although the lodge gateposts survive. To the south of it lay the dairy and model farm. Here Miss Coutts kept not only her herd of award-winning cattle, but also her champion pigs, her white Egyptian donkey (presented to her by costermongers) and her prize Anglo-Nubian herd of goats. She strongly supported the keeping of goats by the poor, as they provided milk for children, although she – and contemporary scientists – did not know the added advantage that goat's milk, unlike cow's, is free from the tuberculosis bacillus. Often wandering through the lawns in the 1860s were two llamas, brought from Peru by Miss Coutts' friend, the traveller Spencer St John. Nothing came of her plan to breed them and produce alpaca cloth.

Proceed along and up **HOLLY LODGE GARDENS**. Set along the opposite side, the substantial houses, roughcast and white-painted, all have some individuality; most have some black half-timbering. The east end of the road is the former "Broad Walk". **No.8** was the home of E J Chapman, composer and one-time Director of Music at Highgate School. Between **Nos.9&10** a passage leads to **No.9A**, which was originally constructed from an outhouse of No.11 Holly Terrace. Harold Evans, then *Sunday Times* editor, lived at **No.11** with his first wife Enid in the 1970s. **No.13** was the home of the scientific-instrument maker Robert Stuart Whipple before his move to Old Hall (p 28) on South Grove. The flats of South Grove House can be seen rising above the house. In front, on its own circular plot, is a splendid ginkgo (maidenhair) tree; it has been considered the third best in the country.

The area on the right was a flower garden in the 19th century and is still used as such. The elegant wrought-iron gate, decorated with black bunches of grapes and gold leaves and supported by brick pillars, once stood in the north wall of the orchard, south of the Robin Grove entrance. It has four stone plaques, two recording its move in 1925, and two recalling the property's former owners – Thomas Coutts in 1819 and Angela Burdett-Coutts in 1869, when she had the orchard wall rebuilt.

West-facing **No.16**, at the top of the rise, was home to Denis Healey, the Labour politician, who moved here from Langbourne Avenue (p 109) with his family c.1957. His wife Edna became interested in Angela Burdett-Coutts, later writing a biography of her called *Lady Unknown*. Edna wrote that the Estate "was like a friendly village". The house cost £7,000 and Denis remembers his time here as probably "the happiest days of our lives". When in 1964 he became Secretary of State for Defence, the family moved to a flat in Admiralty House, letting No.16 to

American friends; they were not to return.

Holly Lodge Gardens rounds the corner to the right. In the 1930s Sir Alfred Brown was living on the left at **No.18**. He was Principal Assistant Treasury Solicitor; after WWII, instead of retiring, he became the legal adviser to the British Military Governor in Germany.

A few metres down, the road becomes **HILLWAY**. This is the spine of the Estate. Its houses are substantial and quite imposing, displaying a variety of mock-Tudor details. Large **No.99**, the first house on the right, is unusual in being built in red brick and in a rather different style. In the wide grass verges that are such an attractive feature of the Estate, forest trees were planted initially but became too large for their purpose. Lime trees are pollarded to keep them under control; laburnums have proved unsuitable and are gradually being replaced by whitebeam.

London is spread out in front of us as we walk down the hill. There is a conveniently sited bench on the left-hand side from which one can take in the view (although luxuriant lime trees obscure the vista from here in summer months). The 'Gherkin' and the London Eye are usually clearly visible.

The upper reaches of Hillway cover the route of old Bromwich Walk, a footpath that bisected the Coutts' estate. It began by the side of South Grove House and ran down to the foot of the hill just east of the

junction of Swain's Lane and Highgate Road (at the end of this route). Originally a field path, it was already an old public track when the Coutts bought the land in 1815. Well defined on the parish map of 1801, it had been given the name of Bromwich (or Bromwich's) Walk when the land belonged to Thomas Bromwich of South Grove House (p 27). Subsequent attempts by the Coutts family to take over the path were thwarted by St Pancras Vestry. Thomas Coutts built high walls on either side, which he disguised with climbing roses and ivy respectively, hence 'Rose Bower' and 'Ivy Walk' in the grounds. The path itself gained a bad reputation for encouraging 'goings-on' amongst the local youth, and the Baroness demanded that the Vestry light the path at night. At last, in 1904, she was able to purchase the path and close it, in return for giving up other land for a widening of Swain's Lane (p 109).

Continue downhill. To our left once lay the kitchen garden of Holly Lodge; the garden of **No.88** has trees from Miss Coutts' 'wooded glade' and that of **No.64** incorporates part of her rockery. First, pass **No.96**, the home until his death in 1941 of James Pinkerton Gilmour, editor of the *Pharmaceutical Journal*. At **No.93** (on the right) the athlete Christopher Brasher (1928-2003) was a registered elector at his parents' home in 1956, the year of his gold-medal triumph in the 3000-metre steeplechase at the Melbourne Olympics.

John Thomas Keep, the founder of a firm of ink manufacturers that still bears his name, died aged 95 in 1965 at **No.87**. Dr Marjory Warren CBE (1897-1960), a geriatrician who did pioneering work at the West Middlesex Hospital, lived at **No.73** until her death in a car accident in France. Sir Graham Wilson, the bacteriologist, was a 1960s resident at **No.65**.

Pause at the junction with **OAKESHOTT AVENUE**. Its name commemorates John Oakeshott, a surgeon who was the medical officer of health for Hornsey and a committee member of the HLSI, and who lived in Feary's Row (p 36) in the 1870s. To the right, the road was laid out over 'Honeysuckle Walk', below which was the site of the Coutts's orchard. Down on the right is **No.9** where the pianist Ernest Henry Lush (1908-88) was living soon after WWII. **No.19** was home from 1937 to the author Stella Gibbons (1902-89) and her second husband, Allan Webb, the actor and singer (d.1959). Her article in the June 1960 edition of the *St Pancras Journal* is a short eulogy on the pleasures of living on such a peaceful Estate, where ducks fly overhead, owls are glimpsed, and hedgehogs come to her back door. She disliked any change to the area, and the Estate has maybe changed less than many other areas because of its privileged privacy. Don't overlook the carefully preserved original electric lamp-posts.

Stella Gibbons is unlikely to have agreed with the verdict of the Camden Association of Architects, who in 1971 gave Holly Lodge Estate a lowly Grade 4 (out of 5), perhaps because of the lack of public facilities mentioned later. They also considered the site had been misused: the grid layout meant that for the most part an "astounding view of London is blocked by the house opposite". At that time about a tenth of the houses on the Estate were occupied by Russians, presumably involved in some way with the Soviet Trade Delegation on Highgate West Hill (p 67). Also living here in the early 1970s, at **No.32**, was Brian Bunting, in exile from his native South Africa, where he was a prominent journalist; he wrote many works opposing the apartheid regime.

Turn left into the eastern end of Oakeshott Avenue, which was laid out on the former outer kitchen garden of Holly Lodge; a gardener's house had stood at this corner. The road is lined on both sides by the tall "mock Tudor cliffs" of **Holly Lodge Mansions**, the first of the flats for lady workers that we shall encounter. They were built in 1925 for Lady Workers' Homes Ltd, which Alderman Abraham Davis had founded in 1914, one of a number of companies and public utility societies that he set up. After the huge losses of men in WWI, many young women were single, and these small bed-sits designed for them were a valued innovation. The single ladies were allowed to buy shares in the company when they moved in. A car was kept at the bottom of the hill to transport them to their homes.

There were 408 bed-sitting rooms in all, some with kitchen alcoves when first built; bathroom and toilet facilities were shared. Both here and in the similar flats in Makepeace Avenue the bed-sitting rooms are gradually being converted into self-contained flats; Camden Council has recently spent £2m converting a block at the end of the street that had been occupied by squatters for many years. Behind the back gardens of the three blocks on the north side runs the wall of the Western Cemetery. The first gate on this side leads to the popular **Holly Lodge Family Centre**, founded in 1990 when a portakabin put up on the site of the original tennis court was taken over. The Holly Lodge Pre-school is also run from here. If the gate is open you can walk along to the entrance of the centre to view the idyllic woodland surroundings of the building and the small playground.

Crossing the road, take the shrub-lined footpath opposite the Centre that runs past the side of the block of flats Nos.211-226. It leads to delightful tiny gardens at the rear. Stay on the footpath under the trees until and then turn left onto an old asphalted path leading into a small rose garden. We are on the site of Traitor's Hill. Here Miss Coutts would bring visitors to admire a wide panorama of London and no doubt relate to them the fanciful story that this was the spot where "Guy Fawkes' fellow conspirators stood waiting to see the Houses of Parliament blown into the air, but the King's troopers, galloping across the open country below from Westminster showed them the plot had failed, and mounting their horses…they fled north to Hatfield." In reality, when the plot was uncovered the conspirators fled separately in different directions.

The site was marked as Traitor's Hill on Rocque's map of 1746. On the 1804 map it is called Prospect Hill, but flanked by Upper and Lower Traitor's Fields. In the map with the sale brochure of 1907 it is again shown as Traitor's Hill accompanied by the story related above. Kite Hill, to the south-west on Parliament Hill, is sometimes also called Traitor's Hill.

Take the asphalt path left out of the rose garden down shallow steps to emerge on a terrace with a view of the lower garden. Continue down the slope to reach a circular pond containing a statue of a young woman holding a book, by an unknown sculptor. On the wall of the basin are four inscriptions. That nearest to us commemorates Alderman Abraham Davis, the founder of Holly Lodge Estate and pioneer of flats for ladies. Walking clockwise around the pond note the three further inscriptions: on the north side to Baroness Burdett-Coutts; on the east to the Directors of the Lady Workers' Homes

Ltd; and on the south an inscription recording the unveiling of the memorial by Alderman Davis' widow on Empire Day in Silver Jubilee year 1935. The statue originally contained a fountain, but it was later vandalised so badly as to be beyond repair. However, local stonemason Fred Pinney very skilfully pieced together the fragments, and the fountain was converted into a pond. The memorial was unveiled a second time in 1992 by Glenda Jackson, the local MP.

From here look east towards the foot of the lawn and the backs of four houses, **Nos.1&2 Hillview** and **Nos.1&2 West View**. Fronting onto Swain's Lane, they were built in 1927 as garages but converted soon afterwards into cottage dwellings. At present they are in keeping with the mock-Tudor style of the Estate. Planning permission was given in 2006 for the replacement of 1&2 Hillview by modernist glass-fronted houses. In early 2007 this was overturned after a mass protest by Holly Lodge Estate residents.

Crossing the grass on the right-hand (south) side of the memorial, and descending steps, follow a pathway between two further blocks of flats, and turn right into **MAKEPEACE AVENUE**. The origin of this name is unknown. The flats here are called **Makepeace Mansions**. 269 bed-sitting rooms were originally built on this east end of the road, c.1925. The post-WWII building across the road,

architecturally much out of keeping with its neighbours, was built by Camden Council to replace the early Restaurant Block. The ground floor of this was a restaurant, primarily for those without kitchen facilities. Social activities were provided above it in reading- and rest-rooms. The block also housed a little theatre called The Little Gem, for several decades the home of the Holly Lodge Dramatic Society, which flourished from the early 1930s until the 1970s. Several other clubs flourished here in the 1930s, including a Youth Club. During the war the building continued in use as a restaurant, but afterwards, as the lady workers got older, the block fell into disuse. When Camden Council became the owners in 1965, they proposed demolishing the block, replacing it with 19 flats, garages and a children's playground. Although such change of use was a breach of the Estate covenants, it was approved by the Lands Tribunal, and 25 flats for old people, with communal facilities, to the designs of John Chandler, were eventually built in 1975-78. The present building also houses the small **Holly Lodge Community Centre**, whose varied activities include a luncheon club for local elderly people. A minibus provides transport to the local supermarket, quite a change from that once provided for the lady workers. The Community Centre provides the only focal point for inhabitants of the Holly Lodge Estate, which otherwise lacks the usual amenities such as schools, churches, playgrounds or sports grounds associated with similar planned developments.

Walk up to the junction with Hillway. Ahead, the western half of Makepeace Avenue comprises a mix of detached and semi-detached houses. **No.5** was the 1970s home of Dr Malcolm Carruthers, a lecturer at St Mary's, Paddington and author of *The Western Way of Death*. George Benson (1911-83), the comedy actor on stage and screen, lived at **No.20** in the 1960s and 1970s, while Chairman of the Society for Theatre Research. Dick Sharples, the TV scriptwriter, occupied **No.28** in 1991.

Turning left at the crossroads, continue down **HILLWAY** to the next junction and pause. **No.22** (farther down on the left) was home to the anthropologist Mary Douglas, Professor of Social Anthropology at UCL and world-renowned for her studies of ritual. She lived here for almost half a century with her husband James, who was Director of the Conservative Research Centre; he died in 2004. Undaunted by a mugging she suffered in Waterlow Park, Mary remained at No.22 until a year before her death, when she moved to a Bloomsbury flat. Dame Mary Douglas died on 16 May 2007 aged 86, a week after her investiture as a DBE. **No.13** was home to the operatic baritone Denis Valentine Dowling (1910-96).

The houses on the four corners of the intersection with **LANGBOURNE AVENUE** make quite a statement; they are turreted and two of them retain their original weathervanes. The significance of the road's name is unclear; perhaps coincidentally, Langbourne is the City of London ward where Coutts' Bank's first City branch was located. Look right along the Avenue's western half. Living down on the left at **No.18** c.1972 was Frederick Morgan, one of the oldest members of the oldest family in Kentish Town. Adjacent semi-detached **No.16** was home for half a century to Stephen Peet (1920-2005), the documentary film maker who had a long and distinguished career with the BBC, for whom he made the series *Yesterday's Witness*. The previous occupants had been Edna and Denis Healey, who were here with their family (see p 106) from 1948 until they moved up the hill to Holly Lodge Gardens 9 years later. Living at **No.29**, on the opposite side, was Francis Boyd, political correspondent of the *Guardian* who knew the Healeys well. Patricia Young, author and editor of the *Nursing Mirror*, and a leading member of the Holly Lodge Dramatic Society, lived next door at **No.31** in 1973, having moved from Langbourne Mansions, the flats at the east end of the street.

We now turn left to reach them, past a number of houses. Where these give out represents the moment when the owners of the Estate decided that the original plan for a house-only development could not be realised, because of the cost of sewers and drainage for the houses at the top of the hill in Holly Lodge Gardens. The 88 flats of **Langbourne Mansions**, beyond, were the first to be erected on the Estate, in 1924, and have never been altered. As you can see, they were more spaciously laid out than those built later. Note the pleasant gardens fronting Nos.9-16 and Nos.17-24.

At the end of the road, pass through the residents' gate into **SWAIN'S LANE** (see also p 33). To our left the road climbs towards the entrances of the two halves of Highgate Cemetery (p 14). Opposite is the Eastern Cemetery, now masked by the trees planted in its early days in the mid-19th century. The plane trees lining the lane on the west side were planted after the Baroness gave land to widen it in 1904, enabling two vehicles to pass abreast. Turn right and walk south. There are few houses on the west side, which is lined mostly by the side walls and back gardens of Langbourne Mansions. Notice the row of 32 garages intruding into the living space behind them. They were built after WWII by the then owners, the Peachey Property Corporation Ltd, who later sold the flats, in 1965, to Camden Council on a 99-year lease.

These lower acres of the Holly Lodge Estate were known in the 19th century as the Home Meadows. In the early days of her ownership Miss Coutts had asked Charles Dickens to look for some land she might give as an open space for the local people. He may have suggested to her the land that is now the Eastern Cemetery. As Mary Howitt recorded in her autobiography, she spent an evening with Miss Coutts in 1855, when the latter confided her frustration about the extension of the cemetery. "A few years ago, she told me, she offered to buy this very land [where] she was intending to make beautiful gardens, to be secured for the public for ever. At the time the proprietor refused to sell; and she naturally feels ill-used." (The proprietor was Harry Chester, who sold the land to the London Cemetery Company.) The land we are passing on the right was an area set aside by Miss Coutts, again on the advice of Dickens, from her estate. Here were entertained large groups of schoolchildren and working-class adults who arrived on horse-drawn wagons on their country outings. The Home Meadows continued to be used for this purpose after the death of the Baroness. Mr Seaton, the editor of the *Hampstead and Highgate Express*, described a walk through the estate in 1911: "they came to Traitor's Hill… In the Home Meadows close at their feet were parties of schoolchildren and mothers' meetings…and in the cricket field adjoining, a vegetable show was being held…reminding us of an old country fair".

Stop where Chester Road (p 100) intersects from the left, and look to the right along **BROMWICH AVENUE**; the spire of St Anne's closes the view. The road has a mixture of smaller detached and semi-detached houses, with attractive rounded covered porches and long gables. The road took its name from Bromwich Walk (p 106). Together with the lower end of Hillway, the Avenue was the first road to be built on the Estate. All the Estate entrances were originally open, but when outsiders started using Bromwich Avenue as a short cut to Hampstead Heath, the London Building Company decided to shut off the roads. The mayor at the time (who lived on the opposite side of Swain's Lane) sought an injunction to stop them, but the company succeeded in installing gates overnight before the court case could be heard; they were allowed to remain. Residents received keys. Visiting charwomen named the Estate "the monkey cage", and it was only after WWII that the pedestrian gates were left unlocked. In the third house on the right, **No.19**, Dr Sam Aaronovitch, economist, author, and campaigner against American comic books, lived in the 1950s and 1960s; his son David (b.1954) is a journalist and regular broadcaster. In his last years, the musician Pasquale Troise (1895-1957) lived at **No.13**. He was the leader of 'Troise and his Mandoliers', who played regularly on *Music While You Work* on BBC Radio. His gravestone in St Pancras Cemetery is in the form of a mandolin.

Across **SWAIN'S LANE** is **Holly Village**, still protected by a fence of diagonal rustic trellis – the height of fashion in 1865 when the village was built for Miss Coutts by her favourite architect, Henry Darbishire. This 'estate' village was in keeping with the model farm and the goats grazing in the Home Meadows, and reflected the image of a rural idyll that the wealthy liked to project on their estates at the time. In December 1903 – a sign of increasing financial difficulties – Baroness Burdett-Coutts had to mortgage Holly Village, along with Nos.5-57 Croftdown Road (p 114), for £15,000; this was only redeemed following their sale in the 1920s, along with the rest of the estate. In 1922, Mr John Arthur Hilliard, tenant of No.6 since 1918, arranged for the village to be sold to the residents for the sum of £6,700. A year later they formed a residents' association, calling themselves the Holly Village Freeholders.

It has often been said that the village was built for the staff of Baroness Burdett-Coutts, although this is belied by contemporary newspaper reports. In the *Illustrated Times* of 21 October 1865 the development is described as "a cluster of pretty cottages…suitable for clerks, commercial travellers and so on, the class of persons for whom they have been designed". Census returns and other sources confirm that the inhabitants, from the earliest days, were not working-class; they kept servants, although usually only one. Tenancies were yearly. In the 1950s, it was still predominantly lower middle-class – a chemist, several clerks, and a 'White Russian' couple of refugees. Only after 1960 did it move upmarket.

Cross over to the entrance of the village, noting the abundant bushes of holly (of both the common and prickle-free Highclere varieties) and of privet to protect the privacy of the residents. Walk up to the archway of the 'monastic Gothic' gatehouse between the two houses, Nos.1&2. Around the arch, inscribed in the stonework in Gothic lettering, are the words "Holly Village erected by A G B Coutts 1865". On either side is a statue of a woman; that on the left (the Good Shepherd) holds a lamb, while that on the right (the Holy Spirit)

clasps a dove. According to Edna Healey, they may represent Miss Coutts and her friend Hannah Brown respectively. Note, too, the small female head in wood by the gatepost, which may also represent the Baroness.

As the estate is private, it is difficult to get a really good view of the 12 houses, arranged around lawns on a triangular site – four detached, eight semi-detached, all in the *cottage orné* style but with different ground plans. Holly Village was Listed Grade II in 1954. A side view is possible by walking a short distance along Chester Road to a sturdy, well-made wooden gate with Gothic details, bearing a carved wooden head, apparently a Green Man.

This gate leads to **No.12** and is sufficiently close to one of the corners of the house for one to see the elaborate detailing of the façade. This was home to the actress Eleanor Bron in the early 1960s and to the singer-songwriter Lynsey de Paul in 1984. Unseen behind is **No.11**, home in 1991 to the architect William Dixon. Return to Swain's Lane, noticing the heads of two men and two women supporting the wooden oriel window on the upper floor of **No.1**, just before the corner. Bearing left past the village entrance, look out for the four gargoyles of animal heads protecting the roofs of the bay window overlooking the front garden of **No.2**. This house was the home in 1890 of John Orleber Payne (1836-1911), a writer on English Catholic history whose works included *Old English Catholic Missions*.

Continue south down Swain's Lane to a second entrance to the Village at the next corner, just beyond **No.4**, where the manager of the Brookfield Stud (p 119, see **[29]**) was living in 1901. Note the decorative heads on either side of the gate and look along the driveway that runs through the back of the village. Anthony Buckeridge (1912-2004), author of the *Jennings* boys' books, once lived briefly at **No.5**. Elizabeth Read, a teacher at Henrietta Barnett school, who in 1973

29 The Brookfield Stud: main stable and riding school, c.1900

ROUTE **6**

wrote an article on Baroness Burdett-Coutts for the first *Camden History Review*, lived at **No.6**. Listed at the same address in the 1881 census was Gerald Sinclair Hayward (1845-1926), the Ontario-born painter in miniature of political figures and celebrities; he was in England for four years until 1883. His neighbour at **No.7** was the portrait painter Frederick Waddy, whose subjects included the novelist Wilkie Collins. In the mid-1970s Maurice (now Lord) Saatchi lived in the house. Henry Beves, a minister of the Catholic Apostolic Church, was listed in the 1921 directory at **No.8**. The driveway offers a splendid example of a Victorian shrubbery.

In stark contrast next door on the left is **No.38 Brookfield Park**. This was built from 1955 on the site of Holly Village's former tennis court, which had been bombed in WWII. The land had been sold to a local GP, previously a tenant of No.6, and the house and surgery was designed for him by the Austrian architect Josef Berger (1897-1989). The tennis court had been part of a Lower Drying Ground (usually referred to as the Drying Green by the residents); the remaining land was developed as garages in 1959. The Upper Drying Ground had been sold in the early 1920s by the newly formed Holly Village Freeholders to the Borough of St Pancras, who incorporated it into the new Brookfield Estate behind, although a small part was retained within Holly Village.

Walk ahead along Brookfield Park (p 114), and shortly turn left at the next crossroads along **ST ALBANS ROAD**. This was named in memory of the Duke of St Albans, the second husband of Harriot Mellon, whose lands Miss Coutts inherited upon his death in 1849. Past an open area on the left with a row of garages built on Holly Village's 'Drying Green', we enter an area of social housing inspired by the garden city movement. After WWI there was a shortage of decent working-class housing, and a cry went up for the building of 'homes for heroes' for the men who came back from the war. Under the Addison Act of 1919, local authority housing was subsidised for the first time. The land here had been purchased by Miss Coutts to protect her Holly Lodge land from any plans to enlarge Highgate cemetery. In 1922 it was bought from the Coutts estate by St Pancras Council, which secured other land at the same time by buying the adjoining Two-Acre Field.

The **Brookfield Estate** was built between 1922 and 1930. The architect was Albert Thomas, who was Edwin Lutyens' office manager from 1902 to 1935. The influence of Lutyens is very apparent. The leaflet produced by the Friends of Highgate Library for their exhibition celebrating Highgate New Town in 2002 describes it as "an estate laid out like a garden suburb". The privet hedges do remind one of Hampstead Garden Suburb and the sloping site, the curving road ahead and mature plane trees all add to the effect. Each property was provided with a fair-sized garden, reflecting the contemporary belief that it was important for working men to remain in contact with the land. The 2-storey cottages (four or six apartments in brick and render) "show the influence of Lutyens' vernacular side".

Pass **KINGSWEAR ROAD** (on the right), which has similar cottage-style properties; as you glance along the road, note the outsize chimney breasts that straddle the ends of the cottages in rural fashion. Kingswear is a Devonshire village linked by ferry to Dartmouth, and the street name reflects the past landowner, the Earl of Dartmouth, who sold this area of his estate for building land. Developed in 1922, the road was known as Linden Road before the houses were built.

Walk ahead to the T-junction with **CROFTDOWN ROAD**. Standing in the railed road island, you are surrounded by blocks of neo-Georgian flats in red brick. Flats were included in the Brookfield Estate scheme to offer affordable housing to poorer families at a time before there was help with rent payments. These 3- and 4-storey neo-Georgian blocks of flats**,** in red brick with stone detailing show the influence of Lutyens' classical side, according to the Friends of Highgate Library. "The fine proportions, attention to detail and careful massing of the chimneys also owe much to Lutyens."

Look left, with the dome and lantern of 'Holy Joe's' just visible above the trees on the horizon. At this end of Croftdown Road, more blocks on the right face others on the left; then the playground and buildings of Brookfield Primary School (p 100), and eventually the side of Highgate Library (p 98) on the corner with Chester Road. At **No.89C**, on the left side and overlooking the school, lived Eric Batson, the early Secretary of the Shaw Society, founded in 1941 on the 85th birthday of the playwright, who made it quite clear he wanted nothing to do with it.

Now turn right along Croftdown Road, crossing over from the road island to its left-hand side, by the block of flats, **No.118A-H**. Emerging beyond is all that remains of an ancient track that once continued westwards to emerge into Highgate Road behind the Bull and Last pub. It still runs north from here, through Highgate New Town, where we encountered it on Route 5 (p 98).

Continue around the bend, past the south end of Kingswear Road (right) and the last row of rural-style cottages on the left. The housing on this side covers the site of the allotments provided by the Baroness in 1876 but closed by her widower in 1913, as was part of the footpath a year later. South of the allotments stood a tennis club **[30]**, with a pavilion built in 1885 by the firm of Cook. Tennis was 'all the rage' in the early 20th century, and the tennis club was a centre of social life for many of the affluent young of neighbouring Dartmouth Park. There are still tennis courts here, beyond the bowling-green on your left, and owned by the Kenlyn Lawn Tennis Club. This shares its facilities with the **Mansfield Bowling Club**, a body of some importance in the world of bowls, which has been a limited company since 1920. Its original clubhouse, built in 1911, has been replaced and has been used by several freemason's lodges. Until recently it housed the temporary HQ of the Honourable

30   The Coutts estate from the south-east, c.1903. The photograph must have been taken from the top of a house in Dartmouth Park Avenue. In the foreground are Miss Coutts' allotments and tennis courts, bounded by a fence along the ancient track which later became the eastern end of Croftdown Road. Beyond, on the left is the Brookfield Stud, above it the church of St Anne's Brookfield. To the right, a glimpse of roofs in Holly Village, and beyond are the extensive grounds of Holly Lodge. The house itself is not visible.

Fraternity of Ancient Freemasons which despite its name was founded by and for women in 1913. The entrance to the two clubs lies between the blocks of 3-storey town houses called **Regency Lawn**, a few metres further on. The houses were flooded soon after they were built in two stages in 1971 and 1973, when the culverted Highgate arm of the River Fleet, which crosses beneath Croftdown Road at this point, overflowed.

Continue across York Rise on the left. When first laid out as a straight turning off Highgate Road, Croftdown Road was a cul-de-sac ending at **No.52** on the south (left-hand) side. The road was begun in 1879 by the local builder Robert Smerdon for Henry Gotto, the owner of Croft Lodge in Highgate Road. The grounds of Croft Lodge, which gave the new road its name, lay between two estates, that of the Earls of Dartmouth to the south and that of Miss Coutts on the north side; the latter was not developed until the turn of the century. A few years later the road was extended to the newly laid out Brookfield Park, and a further extension followed when the Brookfield Estate was built in the 1920s.

Continue along the earliest-built south side, where the tall, red-brick, square-bayed houses boast prominent terracotta decoration. Note the floral designs of the plaques, usually featuring a daisy or marigold; Nos.32-36 have Japanese-style chrysanthemum decoration. **No.32** was the birthplace of Archbishop Donald Coggan (1909-2000). He was the younger son of Arthur Coggan, Mayor of St Pancras in 1912-13 and once national president of the Federation of Meat Traders; his local business connections were with the Lidstones firm. Donald was appointed Archbishop of York in 1961, presided over the writing and publication in 1970 of the New English Bible and became Archbishop of Canterbury in 1974; he retired six years later.

On the corner with Boscastle Road, pause at **No.26**. This bears a terracotta plaque which dates the buildings: "Croftdown Road NW 1880". The houses here were completed by Smerdon in 1879-80. In the stretch ahead, at **No.2**, the artist Flora Polak was living in 1881 with her art-dealer father and her sister Jeanette, a professional singer. Richard Inwards, who died at **No.6** in 1937 aged 97, had managed mines in South America and Spain and been president of the Royal Meteorological Society; his father was the temperance activist Jabez Inwards.

Cross over to Nos.11-13, a tall pair of red-brick semis with much terracotta decoration. Desmond Taylor (1928-78), chief editor of news and current affairs at the BBC lived at **No.11** in the late 1960s. The buildings to the left as far as Highgate Road are part of La Sainte Union School, and include Croft Lodge on the far corner. We, however, return east along the northern side. Nos.15-49 were built in 1899-1900; the area conservation statement notes that there are "deep recessions between each pair to suggest semi-detached houses". Nos.27-37 have striking checkerboard gables. **No.33** was home c.1973 to the playwright Roy Kendall, who wrote *Body and Soul* and *The Perfect Marriage*, a farce in tribute to Ben Travers. A neighbour at about this time was the concert pianist Evelyn Crosland, while John Conteh, the world light-heavyweight boxing champion, was another mid-1970s resident of Croftdown Road. The semis at Nos.53&55 were constructed on a site bombed in WWII; **No.53**, labelled "LSU Provinciale", now houses the offices of the congregation of La Sainte Union.

Continue and eventually turn left into **BROOKFIELD PARK**. The name recalls the meadow through which once flowed the Highgate arm of the River Fleet. The houses here, built mostly by the Smerdon firm, have a distinctly suburban feel. The west (left) side was developed in the years before 1910, except for No.19 which was erected in that year by Grace and Nash. The earlier 3-storeyed houses by Robert Smerdon reflect the influence of the Arts and Crafts Movement and vernacular design inspired by Norman Shaw. The same can be said of the 2-storeyed houses on the opposite side of the road, where **Nos.10-24** were built in 1913 and **Nos.26-32** a year earlier. These were erected by H

E and Frank Smerdon, Robert's sons, who also built **Nos.21&23** on the west side. Bernard Donoughue, the political adviser to Prime Minister James Callaghan, and later Lord Donoughue, lived at **No.7** in 1980. **No.18** was home c.1973 to the artist and illustrator Alan Aldridge, who worked on the *Beatles' Illustrated Lyrics*. Esther Kreitman (d.1954), who wrote stories of Jewish life in London, was another Brookfield Park resident. **No.34** (at present painted a mellow yellow) extends for some distance around the next corner into St Albans Road (see also pp 112, 116).

Pause at the crossroads. Here there was once a fishpond, formed by the River Fleet, lying at the east end of the large garden of Kentish Town House. The house itself fronted Highgate Road. The estate on which it was built was known as Deaconsfield in the 15th century and as Dicas Field in the 17th. Originally copyhold land of the Manor of Cantelowes, it had once been owned by William Bruges (1375-1450), the first Garter King of Arms, and later by the Ive family. John Draper, a London brewer, had his home here in the 16th century. Then, about 1777, a London solicitor called Gregory Bateman built a mansion here which he called Kentish Town House **[31]**. It was later known as Bateman's Folly because

he was ruined by the extravagant building costs. Robert Milligan, the promoter of the West India Docks, was the owner in 1800. A contemporary parish map showed the estate extending east as Cottage Field, which was separated from the house's garden by the river. (This field is now taken by No.38 Brookfield Park and the nearby garages that we passed earlier.) The estate was subsequently bought by Philip Hurd, a

31 'The elegant villa of the late Gregory Bateman at Kentish Town', 1792; otherwise Kentish Town House or Bateman's Folly (Wallis Bequest)

rich lawyer and distinguished art and rare book collector, who was here until 1831. He ran it as a small farm, with piggeries and a dairy, and deer in the grounds. The whole property was bought in 1850 by Miss Coutts, who soon afterwards pulled down Kentish Town House.

Established on part of the site in 1883 was the Brookfield Stud farm, the brainchild of her husband, who ran it very much as an expensive hobby; some thought that there were better uses for his wife's money. Here was bred Sultan, one of the most famous steeplechasers of all time. The Stud specialised, however, in Old English breeds and especially the high-stepping 'Hackney' carriage-horse. Such details emerge from *The Brookfield Stud of Old English Breeds of Horses* that Mr Burdett-Coutts published in 1891 and which was really an advertising brochure for the stud. He [32] also owned Pursley farm, just south of Shenley in Hertfordshire.

There he kept brood horses and grew crops, including hay for the horses at the Stud, while keeping the Pursley farmhouse for his own use. The Stud survived until competition from the motorcar put it out of business in 1910. Here at the east end of the site were the Stud's riding-school ([29], p 111), its granary buildings and the 'covering shed', where mares were mated with stallions.

Now turn left along the western end of **ST ALBANS ROAD**, passing through

32 'The Baroness's Husband' (William Ashmead Bartlett), caricature by 'Spy' (*Vanity Fair*, 12 March 1881)

what was the central area of the Stud grounds. They stretched as far west as the present No.18 on the north side and Coutts Crescent on the south, past which we continue (and to which we shall later return). The main stables occupied the land now covered by the houses on the south side. The opposite side was taken up by the showground, a semi-circular space surrounded by a curving row of 27 loose-boxes. When St Albans Road was eventually extended through the Stud, the main stable-block became the Brookfield Garage (with just one petrol pump), here until 1986.

The road began in the 1850s as a side turning out of Highgate Road. Horace Jones (1819-87), who later became architect to the City of London, designing several of its large market buildings as well as Tower Bridge, had grand plans for the road but built only two houses on the north side and six on the south. Of the latter, three survive beyond Coutts Crescent – Listed **Nos.9-11**, built in 1852 for his daughters by the steelmaker Sir Henry Bessemer, who then lived nearby in Charlton House, on the site of La Sainte Union. Designed by Jones "to appear as one house", the building is in a coarse Italianate style, replete with outsize brackets, and the centre of the façade encloses a large window with side panels of curved plate glass. Look for the decorated panels below the second-floor windows.

No.7, with stucco dressings, relates in design to its neighbours, but with much less bravado, and was once one of a pair. The adjoining No.5 was demolished when Art Deco **Hylda Court** was built alongside. This is a pleasant building of five stories with metal windows, the architecture of which would have been considered very modish when it was built in the early 1930s. An immense willow tree stands in its forecourt.

In the early years of the 20th century Henry E Goodison (p 60) was living at The Hollies, demolished No.3. Former No.1, named Avalon, was home before and during WWI to Thomas Idris, Mayor of St Pancras (1903-04) and founder of the famous soft drinks company. At this time he also had a house on West Hill (p 83). Avalon was then acquired by the Mayoress of St Pancras for use as a Home for Sick Poor Children, opened by Princess Arthur of Connaught in July 1918. A St Alban's Welfare Centre, run by the LCC, was later installed at the same address. The building fell victim to WWII bombs, and **St Albans Health Centre**, its present-day successor, occupies part of the post-war development on the right-hand corner ahead.

Look across to the north side of the road. The only 19th-century houses here are semi-detached **Nos.2&4**, red-brick and stucco villas built by Horace Jones and originally called The Cedars (the name still incised on the stone piers at the entrance)

and The Limes. No.4 gained a 1980s addition and the whole is now called Heath Lodge. No.2 was the 1940s home of Sir Alexander Mackenzie Livingstone, who had been a Liberal MP in the 1920s before defecting to the Labour Party. To the right are Nos.6-18, built in the early 20th century, and all with small details of their own. **No.16** was built by Smerdon Bros in 1910. Tile-hung **No.18**, which abuts it, was erected a year later by a builder not usually associated with Camden, W S Sharpin of Wellington Works, Bow.

Now return east along St Albans Road, noting the present buildings on the former Brookfield Stud site. The houses on the north side **Nos.20-34** were built by Smerdon Bros, some apparently during WWI. Opposite is **Coutts Crescent**, covering the site of the last Stud buildings to disappear. A shallow post-modern arc of striped brick, it comprises nine town houses plus two studio-houses in the tower-like wings, with double-height bedrooms. Built in 1986-89 by Chassay Last Architects, the Crescent was designed to complement the suburban streetscape. An early resident was Sir Kenneth Robinson (1911-96), who succeeded Edith Summerskill as Minister of Health in Harold Wilson's administration, and was MP for St Pancras North from 1949-70. He later served as Chairman of the Arts Council.

Past Coutts Crescent, and occupying the west end of the riding-school site,

are **Nos.25-33**, built by Smerdon Bros c.1911-12, soon after the sale of the Stud. Semi-detached, and with square bays in an Arts and Crafts style, they have unusual front doors with leaded windows on either side, and all have shutters. On the opposite (north) side, at **Nos.36-40**, is a terrace of town houses dating from the 1970s. The larger houses have three long narrow windows on the first floor, the smaller only two. During WWII there was a temporary ambulance station here.

Returning to the Brookfield Park junction, note the Brown House (**No.35**) on the right-hand corner. Built just before WWI, this is an example of an early-20th-century 'butterfly' house, so called from the way the wings are splayed out, but it has been much altered. Turn left and retrace your earlier steps along the north end of Brookfield Park.

We now rejoin **SWAIN'S LANE**. This bears westward hereabouts, and it has been suggested that in the distant past, the original lane – an access track between the fields to the north – was extended from here to the foot of West Hill, following the bank of the River Fleet branch. A track may also have led across the brook and continued southwards to meet up with the ancient footpath that is now College Lane at the top of Grove Terrace in Kentish Town. From the late 18th century the westernmost stretch of Swain's Lane ran alongside the grounds of Kentish Town

House (p 115), and in the early 19th century there were some outbuildings here, pulled down when the estate was sold. The modern town houses at **Nos.46-54** are of a piece with those recently observed in St Albans Road. Beyond them are houses built by Smerdon Bros just before WWI on the north side of the Stud property – **Nos.32-44** in 1914, **No.30** in 1913 and **No.20** and **No.28** in 1912. The remaining houses on this side are of mixed dates and styles and were mostly built between the wars.

Cross over to the north side of Swain's Lane, here lined by houses on the southern boundary of the Holly Lodge Estate, semi-detached and very similar to those around the corner in Hillway. When the Baroness held the land, this was a cricket field below the Home Meadows. The main entrance to the Holly Lodge Estate is next to **No.27**. This is where the car waited to transport the lady workers (p 107) up the hill on their return home. Also here, in the early days of the estate, was a sentry-box occupied by a man dressed in a jacket and brown breeches and a brown bowler hat; his duty was to scrutinise entrants and "to discourage the less than worthy".

Opposite are **No.26**, in a box-like Modernist design, and **Nos.22&24**, a red-brick modern property of the Cambridge-based Circle 33 Housing Association. Its façade has quite attractive windows, but the front garden area is given over to car parking, as are several adjoining front gardens.

We have now reached the small Swain's Lane shopping centre. Its 3-storey buildings, with flats above the shops, have Arts and Crafts black timbers on the façade, linking them with the Holly Lodge Estate. Well patronised by local people, this remains a pleasant place to stroll through, because of the variety and individuality of the shop windows. Cafés make full use of the wide pavements for their tables and chairs.

Farther along on the south side, behind an untidy parking area, is **No.16**, a run-down, seemingly Art Deco building with windows built into its rounded corners. The outside is decorated in two shades of green that were popular in the 1930s, when this building was occupied by Lascotape Ltd, makers of advertising tying-tape. Its walls might benefit today from the attention of its 1953 occupants, the National Association of Operative Plasterers. In the late 1950s No.16 housed the British Syrian Mission, succeeded by the Lebanon Evangelical Mission.

Next are the earliest buildings in this lower part of Swain's Lane, two pairs of semi-detached stuccoed houses built by Griffith Thomas in the early 1850s. They then fronted what was a very narrow lane, not widened until after 1904. They overlooked Miss Coutts' estate and were consequently known as Nos.1-4 Holly Lodge Villas. Nos.12&14 survive in their original form. **No.10** was replaced after the WWII with a modern building that

has nothing to do with the earlier houses. At No.6 is the modern **West Hill House Business Centre**, whose occupants include the British Psychoanalytic Council, and the London Association of Primal Psychotherapists, the latter founded in 1986 to offer psychotherapy to professionals. Beyond, at **Nos.2,4&6A**, are three small, oddly shaped single-storey shops.

On the north side, opposite Nos.8&10, is the southern entrance to the old Bromwich Walk (see p 106), here now called **Church Walk** as it leads to a row of houses built on the land belonging to St. Anne's church. These were built on the site of the church hall, which was used by the Holly Lodge Dramatic Society in its final years. **Nos.1-5** form a terrace of houses with stucco bands and a mansard roof that was added to St Anne's Close (p 83) in the 1980s and is preceded by a row of garages that extend over the small back gardens of the terrace. Church Walk ends at a fence and gated entrance to "private grounds", with a notice that entry is for St Anne's Close residents only. On the east corner of Bromwich Walk is a small wedge-shaped shop with a small window; peer in to view the variety of second-hand goods on sale here in aid of St Anne's Church.

On the other side of Church Walk, at **Nos.1-11A Swain's Lane** and extending to the corner with West Hill, is a line of single-storey shops regarded by the Area Conservation Committee as making a positive contribution to the environment. They are attributed to Alderman Davis as architect and occupy the former garden of St Anne's vicarage. There is now a good mix of well-stocked independent shops. The view is enhanced by the spire of St Anne's church that soars in the background. Despite local protest, **No.1** on the corner, the longstanding hardware shop of A H Lever and Son (*alias* Cavours Hardware) closed in March 2007. The owner, Lord Listowel, wished to demolish the parade and replace it with a 3-storey block, although he withdrew the plans in the face of fierce local opposition. In the summer of 2007 the shop was taken over as a temporary art gallery by a Highgate-based collective called the Artists Liberation Front, aiming to strike a blow at sale fees charged by expensive West End galleries. The shop is embraced on two sides by a restaurant with a second frontage in Highgate West Hill. This was built as a branch of Barclays Bank in 1929, and its closure in 1990 was a lamented loss of banking facilities for local people.

On the opposite corner stands the **Duke of St Albans**. A pub has stood here since the mid-19th century, when it was owned by Watney, Coombe & Reid. It was rebuilt in 1953 after war damage. Known for a few years more recently as the Platinum Bar, it reverted to its original name in 2003, when the interior was refurbished in a more traditional style. The name commemorates the 9th Duke of St Albans, the second husband of Harriot Mellon, the early owner of Holly Lodge.

As the end of our walk approaches, we have returned to the junction that John Betjeman thought of as the beginning (or end) of London. Turn left into **HIGHGATE ROAD**. Here the 'Parliament Hill Fields' bus stand cuts into the frontage of **Nos.37-61 St Albans Villas**, a block of council flats built on a bombed site by St Pancras Council a few years after the present pub. The flats preserve the name of the mid-19th-century houses at the front of the former Kentish Town House estate. The original Nos.10-14 St Albans Villas stood north of St Albans Road, while Nos.1-9 lay beyond. Nos.7-9 on the far corner were bombed during WWII, and are now covered by further post-war flats, **Nos.7-12** and **Nos.13-36 St Albans Villas**. The remaining houses survived the war. Nos.3-6, now known as **Nos.3-6 Oak Court**, are linked semi-detached villas with Ionic pilasters and heavily rusticated ground floors. No.4 St Albans Villas (now **No.4 Oak Court**) was home to Thomas Idris (see p 83) before he moved round the corner into St Albans Road (p 117). Beyond, and fronting a further block of post-war flats (**Nos.62-69**) are **Nos.1-2 St Albans Villas**, original houses retaining their old name. Shapurji Saklatvala, the Bombay-born Communist politician, lived at No.2 until his death here of a heart attack in 1936. For most of his parliamentary career from 1924 to 1929, he had been the sole Communist representative in Parliament. From 1938 until the outbreak of WWII, the same house was home to Paul Robeson, the singer, actor and political activist, with his wife Essie (Eslanda), who managed his career. During this period he performed without fee at the left-wing Unity Theatre in Somers Town as an ordinary member of the cast despite being an international superstar.

Some four centuries have elapsed since the apothecary Thomas Johnson and nine of his botanist friends passed this way. They travelled from the City on 1 August 1629 to Kentish Town, and then walked up to Highgate and on to Hampstead Heath, recording the flowers as they went. Later that year Johnson published the survey (in Latin). This is the earliest known account of such an expedition for scientific purposes in the London area to be published in the British Isles. It was translated into English, with the help of R E Latham, by Richard (R S R) Fitter, who published the book in 1945 when he was living in South Grove House (p 26).

Our walks have shown how this area, despite the development of the land for housing in the 19th and 20th centuries, still retains more of the rural ambience known to Johnson than is now left to most Londoners. Fortunate indeed are the residents of Highgate.

ROUTE **6**

Sources

Books and pamphlets

Baker, T F T (ed.). *A history of the County of Middlesex*, Vol.6 [including] *Hornsey with Highgate*. IHR; OUP, 1971

Barber, Peter (comp.). *Old streets of Highgate*. Lauderdale House Society, 1979

Barber, Peter, Cox, Oliver and Curwen, Michael. *Lauderdale revealed*. Lauderdale House Society, 1993

Barker, H S M & Bruce, J R E F. *St Mary Brookfield centenary 1875-1975*. The church, 1975

Bebbington, Gillian. *London street names*. Batsford, 1972

Braithwaite, Rose May. *Making a Victorian garden*. Hornsey Historical Society, 1994

Bryant, Julius. *Kenwood: the Iveagh Bequest*. English Heritage, 2005

Burdett-Coutts, B. *The Brookfield Stud of old English breeds of horses*. Sampson Low, 1891

Cherry, Bridget & Pevsner, Nikolaus. *London 4: North (The buildings of England)*. Penguin, 1999

Clinch, George. *Marylebone and St Pancras*. Truslove & Shirley, 1890

Cooper, Pam. *Waterlow Park: a garden for the gardenless*. Chico Publications, 2006

Cox, Oliver, Cox, Jean and Watkinson, Fabian. *Lauderdale reborn*. Lauderdale House Society, 2003

Cunnington, Elisabeth and Rust, Frances. *All Highgate is a garden: a history of the Highgate Horticultural Society*. Hornsey Historical Society, 1989

Day, Sidney. *London born*. Harper Perennial, 2006

Denyer, C H (ed.). *St Pancras through the centuries*. Le Play House Press, 1935

8 Stoneleigh Terrace (London Open House factsheet, 2003; researched by Ian Dungavell)

Fairfield, S. *The streets of London: a dictionary…* Macmillan, 1983

Friends of Highgate Cemetery. *In Highgate Cemetery*. Highgate Cemetery Ltd, 2005

Healey, Edna. *Lady unknown: the life of Angela Burdett-Coutts*. Sidgwick & Jackson, 1978

Healey, Edna. *Part of the pattern: memoirs of a wife at Westminster*. Headline Review, 2006

Holly Lodge Estate Committee. *Holly Lodge Estate*. The committee, 1973

Howitt, Margaret (ed.). *Mary Howitt: an autobiography*. The editor, 1889

Jealous, Walter K. *Highgate Village*. Baines & Scarsbrook, 1919

Jealous, Walter K. *Reminiscences of Highgate*. Baines & Scarsbrook, 1902

Jones, Dave. *Hampstead and Highgate tramways*. Middleton Press, 1995

Lee, Charles E. *St Pancras Church and Parish*. St Pancras PCC, 1955

Lewis, C L Mrs. *Dr Southwood Smith: a retrospect*. William Blackwood & Sons, 1898

Lloyd, John H. *The history of Highgate*. Published by subscription, 1888

London County Council. *Survey of London*, Vol.17: *The village of Highgate*. LCC, 1938

McDowall, David & Walton, Deborah. *Hampstead Heath: the walker's guide*. David McDowall, 1998

Miller, Frederick. *St Pancras past and present*. Abel Heywood, 1874

Minney, Sarah K. Exhibition brochure *Slavery and justice, the legacies of Dido Belle and Lord Mansfield*. English Heritage, 2007

Norrie, Ian (ed.). *Heathside book of Hampstead and Highgate*. High Hill Press, 1968

Palmer, Samuel. *St Pancras, being antiquarian… memoranda…* The author, 1870

Pevsner, Nikolaus. *London, except the Cities of London and Westminster. (The buildings of England)* Penguin, 1952

Port, Michael (ed.). *Who built your house?* Dartmouth Park Conservation Area Advisory Committee, 2003

Prickett, Frederick. *The history and antiquities of Highgate*. The author, 1842

Richardson, John. *Highgate: its history since the fifteenth century*. Historical Publications, 1983

Richardson, John. *Highgate past: a visual history of Highgate*. Historical Publications, 2nd edition, 2004

Richardson, John. *A history of Camden*. Historical Publications, 1999

Robeson, Paul Jr. *The undiscovered Paul Robeson*. Wiley, 2001

Ryder, Rowland. *Edith Cavell*. H Hamilton, 1975

Schwitzer, Joan. *Highgate walk no.2*. Hornsey Historical Society, 1983

Schwitzer, Joan. *Highgate walks: a local history guide*. Hornsey Historical Society, 1996

Schwitzer, Joan (ed.). *People and places: lost estates in Highgate, Hornsey and Wood Green*. Hornsey Historical Society, 1996

Schwitzer, Joan & Gay, Ken. *Highgate and Muswell Hill*. Chalford, 1995

Sinclair, Frederick (comp.). *St Pancras through the ages: catalogue of an exhibition*. MB of St Pancras, 1938

Stokes, Malcolm. *A walk along the ancient boundaries of Kenwood*. Hornsey Historical Society, undated

Walton, W A. *Fifty years of North London Bowling Club*. The club, 1941

Weinreb, B & Hibbert, C (eds). *The London encyclopaedia*. Macmillan, 1992

Winser, Ann. *Highgate Road Chapel 1877-1980*. The chapel, 1980

Whittington Hospital History Project. *The hospital on the hill: the story of the Whittington Hospital*. The project, 1992

Whyman, Des. *Shoulder of Mutton Field*. Meath Publications, 2005

Woodford, F Peter (ed.). *A constant vigil: 100 years of the Heath and Old Hampstead Society*. The Society, 1998

Maps

Rocque 1745, Thompson 1801/1804 & terrier map; Davies 1834; Greenwood 1834; Britton 1834; parish 1849 & 1861; Stanford 1862; Cassell 1862; Ordnance Survey 1869 & later; Bacon 1888; Booth's poverty maps 1889–98; LCC bomb damage maps; Corporation of London map of Hampstead Heath.

Index

Streets included in the survey are indicated in boldface, as are the main entries for these and other selected subjects;
* = illustration.

124